About the Author

Gemma Summers PhD is a personal coach and counsellor with an extensive background in training and facilitation. Her consultancy, *Go for Goals,* offers coaching, counselling and conflict resolution services. She lives in Sydney and can be reached through her website at http://www.goforgoals.com.au or via her email at gemma@goforgoals.com.au

How to Get What You Want

without LOSING it

a woman's
guide to
resolving
conflict

GEMMA SUMMERS

BANTAM

HOW TO GET WHAT YOU WANT WITHOUT LOSING IT
A BANTAM BOOK
First published in Australia and New Zealand in 2002
by Bantam

National Library of Australia
Cataloguing-in-Publication Entry

Summers, Gemma.
   How to get what you want without losing it: a woman's guide to
   resolving conflict.
   Bibliography.
   ISBN 1 86325 355 6.
   1. Women – communication – Case studies. 2. Interpersonal
   communication – Case studies 3. Conflict management
   – Case studies. I. Title.
158.2082

Transworld Publishers,
a division of Random House Australia Pty Ltd
20 Alfred Street, Milsons Point, NSW 2061
http://www.randomhouse.com.au

Random House New Zealand Limited
18 Poland Road, Glenfield, Auckland

Transworld Publishers,
a division of The Random House Group Ltd
61–63 Uxbridge Road, London W5 5SA

Random House Inc
1540 Broadway, New York, New York 10036

Typeset by Midland Typesetters, Maryborough, Victoria
Printed and bound by Griffin Press, Netley, South Australia

10 9 8 7 6 5 4 3 2 1

To Arny and Amy Mindell, who taught me that conflict can open the heart, mind and spirit.

Contents

Preface

What makes us happy?

I think happiness is a state of being that occurs whenever we (or those we care about) get what we want. Happiness rises and falls each day as we encounter the world and negotiate our way with others, successfully or not. Often we think of happiness as something that happens to us, if we're lucky enough. We're just passive recipients of this wondrous experience. But is that true? Must we just wait for happiness to land upon our heads? I don't think so. I think we are happy in our lives when we are pursuing what matters to us most and getting what we want.

But what do you want? Big question.

What you want probably changes in each moment as you move through your days and weeks and watch your life unfold. Mostly people want more or less of something: more time, less stress; more courtesy, less rudeness; more money, less struggle; more friends, less loneliness; more recognition, less neglect; more help, less hindrance; more love, less fighting; more leisure, less work; more agreement, less tension; more success, less insecurity; more confidence, less fear. The list goes on and on. What you want may be different in each encounter and in each area of your life. There are the little wants of the moment and the big wants of a lifetime.

Pursuing and getting what we want often means encountering conflict and successfully resolving it. This book is about conflict resolution, a fundamental skill needed by every woman in every aspect of her life – whether at home, at work or in the larger community. These skills are vital for dealing effectively with everyday encounters with others and for successfully pursuing goals and dreams. Conflict is commonly perceived as a difficult event that should be avoided at all costs. But what is truly amazing about conflict is its power to illuminate what we want or care most about in life. It shows us who we are and points to directions for our future, like a compass on the road of life.

To many women, the idea of conflict represents loss. Loss of face, loss of power, loss of emotional control, loss of perspective, loss of relationship, loss of something they want. But here's the good news: deep down, resolving conflict is about creating happiness in our individual lives and in our world. It's about people getting what they want – individually and together. You *can* find a way to resolve conflict and get what you want without losing anything but your fear.

I invite you to come with me now to explore the amazing world of conflict. You will learn how to negotiate your way more successfully in life and create greater happiness for yourself and those you care about.

How to Use This Book

I have written the book in a logical sequence, starting with a general overview of conflict, then getting straight into the four main steps of conflict resolution. I have written it this way so that you can head right to the practical *how to* part of conflict resolution.

However there is another way you might wish to read this book. One of the interesting things about conflict is that although you may know the steps, you might still find you have trouble applying them. Feelings such as fear, anger or confusion seem to prevent you. You may prefer, therefore, to start with chapters that deal with the more emotional issues surrounding conflict; chapters such as Chapter 8, Fear of Conflict, Chapter 9, Developing Clarity, or Chapter 10, Inner Conflict. You can then return to Chapters 3 to 6 for the four main steps.

Finally, the three appendices include a conflict resolution skills checklist to help you gauge your strengths and weaknesses, a step-by-step guide summarising the stages of conflict resolution, and a brief overview of common causes of conflict plus the basic principles that help prevent conflict.

The book is intended as a guide to be used by you as best suits your needs. I suggest you follow your own interest and curiosity, which is always a useful attitude for working with conflict.

Introduction: Why Women Need this Book

*Peace is people talking together with a heart
in between them.*

Child, aged 8

Why write a guide to resolving conflict just for women? After all, there are many books available on how to have more love in your life, how to end the gender wars, how to negotiate better, how to listen better, how to communicate more clearly or compromise more reasonably. But as helpful as these books are, very few of them address the specific needs, issues and talents of women in conflict.

My aim is to help women find their authentic and powerful voice during conflicts with partners, family members, friends, co-workers and even acquaintances. I believe women can learn the art of conflict resolution and negotiation without either sacrificing themselves or damaging their relationships.

I have a deep and abiding interest in helping women understand and use conflict more creatively in their lives. As a social psychologist and personal coach and counsellor, I work with many women who encounter conflict as they navigate their goals in life. I coach them to use the tools of conflict resolution for their own empowerment and life enhancement.

I have always been interested in conflict. This interest eventually led to my undertaking doctoral research on conflict resolution, driven by the twin questions of why is conflict so difficult and how can it be less so. A key mentor in my learning was Dr Arnold Mindell, psychologist and mediator. His approach was based on the idea that conflict is a potentially meaningful and creative event that has the power to transform our lives, our relationships and our communities, if worked with constructively. Conflict is thus an important dynamic of change that can foster our individual and collective growth.

Dr Mindell's positive and yet profound approach to conflict deeply impressed me and I studied and trained in this model for the next ten years. This took me on an adventurous and often demanding journey which included being part of a conflict resolution team, dedicated to the study and application of conflict resolution methods to large-scale social and community conflicts around the world. In places such as Northern Ireland, Slovakia, Switzerland, United States, Canada and Australia we implemented and taught the methods to others. The team continues its work today and is part of a broad international network of people committed to studying and understanding conflict, social change and group transformation.

Mindell's model of conflict resolution, upon which this book is based, has been taught to people all over the world. Its practical applications are broad and diverse, from helping individuals resolve their inner conflicts, to assisting couples to work on relationship tensions, to addressing social and community issues. I have adapted the model to make it relevant to the needs of women wanting to develop greater confidence and self-expression in their daily lives. These tools are powerful aids for any woman wanting to achieve her goals and maintain positive and co-operative relationships with others. In my work as a coach and counsellor over the years I have seen many women transform their lives as they master these tools.

Although the ideas and skills in this book are equally relevant to men and women, I have chosen to focus on women's experience with conflict. I don't think it comes as much of a surprise that conflict affects men and women differently. Most of us intuitively sense that there are some differences in the way men and women perceive and respond to conflict. For instance, many men (though certainly not all) appear to express criticism or anger more freely than do many women, and assert their individual viewpoint more easily. This may be due to the fact that men, generally speaking, tend to perceive relationships in more hierarchical or competitive terms, or because they experience less inner conflict between asserting their individual needs and their identity as a man, or because they possess greater personal confidence due to their higher social status. Women, on the other hand, often feel more vulnerable in the presence of conflict, especially when conflicting with a man, and may even sacrifice their individual needs to maintain the harmony of a relationship or to preserve their sense of security.

Women also talk about conflict differently, focusing more on relational aspects rather than the rational or legalistic aspects more typical of men. Many of these different perceptions of and responses to conflict reflect the different social realities men and women inhabit. Because of these and other differences, it makes sense to focus on the specific challenges and issues women encounter in conflict.

Whenever gender behaviours are described, it is important to remember that these are general patterns only and that individuals vary greatly in their behaviour. In other words, our behaviour is not limited by our gender. We are always free to express and develop ourselves as individuals.

Differences also exist among women, differences that reflect personality type, childhood experiences, culture, socio-economic background and lifestyle. These differences may enable one woman to tackle conflict directly and fearlessly, while causing another to shy away from it or become very emotional. But while acknowledging these many differences, my aim is to address *over-arching* patterns that both advantage and disadvantage women in conflict.

In this book you will read about women like yourself, struggling to deal with the daily tensions with others that are part and parcel of life – and succeeding with the help of the skills in this book. These stories are of women dealing with conflict with intimate partners, female friends, family members and workmates, as well as with their own inner conflicts. These are conflicts we all struggle with from time to time, especially conflicts with intimate partners. I have seen many women struggle, often unsuccessfully, to negotiate their needs and resolve differences with male partners. For this very reason, I use many case studies of conflict between men and women in intimate relationship. Intimate relationships present special challenges. It is where our most private selves are revealed and our deepest needs emerge, and, more often than not, where our most volatile and damaging conflicts occur. This is also true for same-gender relationships. All women, whether heterosexual or lesbian, will benefit from reading this book and strengthening their conflict resolution skills. When our primary relationship is not working, life can feel hopeless and grey. We look to our intimate relationship as a primary source of support, connection and love, so it is vital that this central relationship be able to deal with its differences. The stories are based on actual events. However, the details have been changed to protect the privacy of individuals.

In the world today, however, many women are single, divorced or between relationships. If you're not in a so-called intimate relationship, you no doubt have close friends, relatives and colleagues who provide similar support and meet many of those same emotional needs. Whatever your relationship status, you need conflict resolution tools to maintain your relationships and negotiate your needs, especially within those relationships most central to your life.

Aims of this book

My aims for this book are threefold:
- To provide simple, down-to-earth conflict resolution tools for women.

- To uncover beliefs that prevent women from using these tools and find ways to move beyond these limiting beliefs.
- To affirm the powers and skills women already possess for creating positive negotiation and peaceful change.

Just like learning to read, swim or drive a car, conflict resolution takes practice, but as conflict is a periodic occurrence, there are plenty of opportunities to master these tools. By practising these tools, you will soon know how to negotiate your needs in relationship so that both parties receive maximum support to grow and benefit from the interaction, while minimising losses for each person. You will begin to see conflict as offering useful information for change and will learn to use this information in fair and productive ways. You can now say 'goodbye' to dead-end arguments and 'hello' to understanding and learning. The work you do on conflict, both inner and outer, will make all your relationships healthier, happier and more rewarding places in which to live, work and love.

Part One

The Basic Steps to Resolution

1 Women and Conflict

*Our lives extend beyond our skins, in radical
interdependence with the rest of the world.*

Joanna Rogers Macy

You probably already know a lot about how to handle
conflict. You may even know exactly what you should do
during conflict, such as be more assertive, put aside emotion,
be less afraid and know your bottom line. But despite this
knowledge, you may find yourself unable to do these things
easily or successfully. Why is this? Let's take a look.

One reason is simply that all the best intentions in the world
to become more assertive or effective in conflict won't work if
our identity as women isn't taken into consideration. Whether
this identity is the result of social conditioning, biological,
historical or evolutionary forces, or a potent mix of all these
factors, is a question beyond the scope of this book. What we
can say, however, is that feminine consciousness appears to
be oriented differently in several key ways from masculine
consciousness. One of the most recognised of these differences is
in the realm of relationship. On the whole, women tend to
derive more of their identity from their relationships than do

men. That is, we place a high value on relationship and cultivate those skills that support cohesion and harmony in relationship. Conflict, which is an uncomfortable polarisation of people into different camps, however fleetingly, can threaten this vital sense of comfort and unity found in relationship. Conflict can be seen as a 'breaker' of relationship, a very threatening event.

Without understanding how women perceive and respond to conflict, and where our particular strengths and weaknesses lie, we may not be able to use the many excellent conflict resolution tools available to us. After all, what good is a tool if it is too threatening, awkward or foreign to use?

For instance, some conflict resolution tools can be difficult to use because they conflict with deeply-held beliefs about who we think we are or should be. So if your identity as a woman requires that you never get angry or make another uncomfortable, you might find it hard to use the skill of Taking Your Own Side in a conflict, which requires asserting your own thoughts, feelings and needs.

Asserting your own viewpoint may conflict with your image of yourself as a loving woman. Images of yourself as *nice* or *giving* or *understanding* make it hard to disagree, confront or defend yourself. Likewise, images of yourself as *powerful* or *in control* or *perfect* can make it hard to see someone else's viewpoint. Some communication skills are easy for us to use, some are a little harder.

Fear of conflict

Another powerful barrier to using the tools of conflict resolution is *fear* of conflict. Fear is the most common response to conflict and is an ancient survival mechanism hard-wired into our primitive brains. Fear tells us we are in danger and prepares us for fight or flight. This automatic response can be hard to control when we feel threatened. On top of this ancient reflex, women often have an additional layer of conditioning which tells them it is unacceptable for them to assert themselves or to openly conflict. Or to win.

I understand this fear of conflict all too well. As well as being gentle in nature, I was raised to be a peacemaker, like many women of my generation. I was raised to think that anger was bad, that having a different viewpoint was unfriendly, and that conflict was unbecoming. But despite all my insecurities about conflict, I managed to retain a love of learning and an adventurous streak that wouldn't quit. In some ways, I *have* grown up to be the peacemaker I was encouraged to be, except the difference is that now I use peacemaking skills to work through conflict, not avoid it.

The importance of women's fear of conflict was brought home to me through the conflict resolution classes I taught to women. When I first began teaching, I noticed a few interesting things. I noticed that some skills were easier for women to pick up, skills such as Taking the Other Side, which required listening, empathy and curiosity. Other skills, such as Taking Your Own Side, took a lot more encouragement, due to many women's past negative experiences of conflict, coupled with disempowering beliefs about themselves. They believed they would lose in a conflict, and so they did.

During these classes many women talked about their feelings of apprehension whenever they were faced with a conflict. They were concerned about what was safe or prudent for them to say. Here are some of the concerns they raised:

- How honest can I afford to be?
- What is the cost of sharing my real perceptions and feelings?
- Will there be negative consequences for having a voice?

These fears, though understandable, unfortunately prevent many women from using the tools of conflict resolution. Many women prefer silence as the time-proven and safe method for dealing with conflict. The less said, the less trouble.

But why so much fear? One reason is that women have been raised that way. Society encourages women to 'keep the peace', often at the cost of their own needs and the development of their own voice in the world. Some women have also been hurt in childhood by aggressive adults or siblings and consequently view conflict as a losing proposition. Naturally enough, they want to avoid 'trouble' at all costs. This is a most distressing consequence. Resolving our problems with others requires not avoiding nor smoothing over tensions, but engaging each other in genuine conversation. As fear of conflict is such a central issue in conflict resolution, I have devoted an entire chapter to it in Chapter 8.

Most of us already know about the negative side of conflict and probably have a few war stories to tell about hurtful conflicts in our lives. We probably don't think of conflict as an opportunity for creating positive change. All too often we perceive conflict as a dangerous situation in which we could 'get into trouble' or lose something vital, such as love, power, security or approval. Or just simply lose. For many of us, conflict is an area of vulnerability where we fear loss of face, loss of power or blows to our heart.

Out of our need to protect ourselves from damaging

conflicts, we may decide to steer clear of *all* conflict. When we do this, however, we never learn the value of knowing how to conflict effectively when need be. We never learn how to negotiate our needs and differences fairly, thus losing the opportunity for meaningful exchanges where we don't give ourselves away, dominate others or lose sensitivity.

Many men fear conflict as much as women do. After all, who wants to engage in painful or embarrassing disagreements with others if they can possibly avoid it? Some men are terrified of a woman's emotion and will therefore avoid conflict with her. Avoidance is the first strategy most of us employ when disagreement rears its ugly head. We just look the other way and pretend it isn't happening. If this works, and sometimes it does, great. But avoidance only works some of the time and with some people.

So what do we do with those disagreements and differences that can't be avoided without negative consequences for our relationships, such as a loss of honesty, intimacy or solutions for living or working together happily? What do we do about those differences that when left unresolved eat into our morale, our self-esteem and our dreams for success, love or friendship?

In Chinese the word for 'crisis' has a double meaning. It means both danger *and* opportunity. So it is with conflict. Conflict is a crisis and an opportunity. Though conflict may frighten us, it is also an opportunity to deepen our relationships and create new understanding. Conflict can teach us many valuable lessons if we are open to learning them. Paradoxically, the more we deal honestly with conflict in our lives, facing it with an open heart and desire to learn, the less conflict we will have.

Conflict resolution is an excellent way to resolve differences safely, so that we needn't avoid conflict nor engage in awkward and hurtful fights. To resolve conflict safely, we need to enter it consciously, using effective tools. You can minimise the negative impact of conflict in your life, dissolve trust-eroding tensions with others and increase peace and confidence by practising these safe and gentle techniques.

This book answers women's fundamental questions about conflict:

- How do we resolve our differences without damaging our relationships?
- How do we make the process non-hurtful and enriching?
- How do we learn from our conflicts, so that we needn't repeat them?
- How do we make changes in our lives and relationships based on what we learn in conflict?

Conflict is not the enemy. Conflict will be with us for as long as we are all growing and changing and having differences. Which is to say, forever.

Gender talk

During the 1990s, Deborah Tannen's bestseller, *You Just Don't Understand*, created a sensation by outlining the different and the implicit 'rules' that shape male and female communication. She asserted that women's conversational style reflects their interest in creating and maintaining relationship. Men's conversational style reflects their interest in delivering information and maintaining or improving their position in the male social order. Tannen pithily named these two gender styles Rapport Talk and Report Talk.

Just as men and women often converse differently, men and women often conflict differently. Many men come to the conflict table with their position already firm in their minds, having thought through the matter first. Women often come to the table expecting to discover or develop their position through discussion and mutual exploration. We will discuss these differences in conflict styles in greater depth in Chapter 3, Take Your Own Side, and explore how these differences advantage and disadvantage women in conflict. These disadvantages can be overcome with a little thought and planning, as we will discuss later.

Despite these seemingly unchangeable gender communication styles, new patterns of behaviour can be learned. Not only that, but we now know that specific gender differences once thought to be biological actually reflect learned roles. For instance, extremely deferent or passive behaviour may have still been accepted or even expected in women three or four decades ago, but today these are viewed as negative traits in women competing for a social and economic spot in the marketplace. Expectations of behaviour do change as society changes, although slowly. Too often, men and women take the idea of gender difference as the final word, digging in their heels and refusing to learn or expand their communication repertoire. It's up to us as adults to become whole individuals and stretch ourselves to learn skills that weren't taught to us as children.

Both genders possess communication strengths *and* weaknesses. Instead of clinging to our gender style in defensiveness or creating yet another power struggle over whose communication style shall prevail, we can learn from each other's style.

It's more fun for all of us to cultivate communication skills that include the best of both approaches. After all, men and women have more in common than they have differences. That is one of the most important steps in conflict resolution – noticing and acknowledging commonalities.

We can all learn to listen more, speak more directly, and build more equitable relationships. These days both women and men are learning how to use the two key energies needed for conflict resolution: competing and co-operating. Conflict resolution is a co-operative and non-adversarial approach to solving differences that allows the individuals involved to promote their own needs and interests. Once both sides have asserted their interests, they then co-operate to find a solution together.

Your powerful female skills

It is important to acknowledge the many wonderful inherent skills women possess for dealing with conflict. Women have made enormous contributions to peace and human rights all over the world. They have also spearheaded the 'relationship movement', bringing new ideas for fulfilment and equality within the realm of intimate relationship. Their increased presence in the workforce has helped changed the communication culture of organisations and corporations. Here are some of the skills women naturally possess that are vital to resolving differences and restoring peace:

- active listening
- empathy, care and concern
- openness to learning

- co-operation
- verbal fluency
- psychological flexibility
- emotional honesty
- self-reflection
- intuition and insight
- practicality

Ask yourself:
- How are you using these skills successfully in your life already?
- How do you appreciate these skills in others?
- What other skills do you use for solving conflict?

Knowing what skills you possess empowers you to use them more confidently in your life. We all have our own way, our own unique power and style in conflict. Some woman are commanding warriors who take on battles with lots of fire, others are gentle flowers who approach conflict with a feeling sensitivity that's very powerful. Some women are Zen monks who are focused and to the point in their style. Discovering and proudly owning your unique style gives your conflict resolution skills authenticity. You don't have to be anyone other than who you are to resolve conflict.

Personal conflicts are planetary conflicts

If you think your conflicts are only a private matter, think again: many personal conflicts are also planetary conflicts. Each time you resolve a conflict – whether over money, children, work, relatives, housework, sex, shopping or bills, you are working towards world peace. This may sound like an exaggeration, but it's true! Planetary conflicts are resolved in the same way personal conflicts are resolved – by people coming together to learn about each others' needs. Whether in Sydney, Los Angeles, Belfast, or Auckland people want to be respected and understood. Everyone wants to be heard, whether in their private relationships, in their jobs, by their governments or by other nations. Educating ourselves to solve conflict positively and democratically in our relationships, workplaces, families and local communities builds a solid foundation for a more stable world.

Whenever I work with a woman in a workshop who is struggling with a conflict, other women present in the room always readily understand her issue. They vigorously nod their heads and eagerly offer ideas on how she might move toward resolution. We all struggle with similar issues. Our private conflicts are not unique, even though we may feel isolated in them. This is one of the reasons why self-help groups and books are so popular – they break the isolation of what was once seen as a personal problem or failure.

Story: Freedom to disagree

Conflict resolution is based on the idea that each of us has our own unique perspective and is free to disagree. Sometimes we don't use that freedom. As women, we have often been encouraged to love 'unconditionally', to accept people as they are and not try to influence outcomes. We are not supposed to object, probe or challenge. But inhibiting our self-expression leads to ineffectual communication.

Jill is a sixty-year-old woman who was raised to obey her parents and not question authority. She was trained to think that probing or mistrusting others was unreasonable. To compound matters, Jill and her husband both believed that any trouble in marriage is due to a woman's 'lack of submission'. Jill thought she had to accept her husband as he was and not probe for information, so even when he asked her to co-sign a blank withdrawal slip for their joint bank account, she asked no questions.

Predictably, Jill's husband embezzled their life savings from their account. This disaster might have been prevented had Jill been able to probe and disagree, and if Jill had understood how important it was that she follow her gut instinct and voice her concerns. The marriage may not have been salvageable in the long run, but Jill would have saved her money and her self-respect.

My work with Jill involved helping her identify and question those beliefs which undermined her capacity for honest discussion and which held her back in life. For Jill, as for many women, the big breakthrough came when she saw how little support and training she'd received to take her own side or even to say 'No'. She decided to change this state of affairs by taking active responsibility for all areas of her life.

Jill is now divorced and runs a successful catering business. She has claimed the freedom to disagree and to negotiate her needs with others and has transformed her life as a result.

Being free to disagree, respectfully, is important for keeping relationships healthy and your own self-esteem intact. By learning to resolve conflict, we break the resignation and passivity that holds us in place. This empowers us in all areas of our lives as we learn the fundamental tools for addressing differences everywhere.

Spiritual vision gives us courage

The spiritual vision behind conflict resolution is very simple:

- a commitment to learning about each other and ourselves
- a commitment to democratic methods of resolving differences

This commitment to learning and democracy provides the courage we need to face our conflicts, both inner and outer. Without this deeper vision, it can be difficult to overcome our fears and automatic reactions. Having a higher goal can empower us to step into the uncertain territory of conflict when necessary. Conflict resolution is a path of love and respect, a win–win game where both parties are honoured for their viewpoints and their needs taken into consideration.

Most of us are just beginners at learning how to get along with one another. Having a beginner's mind is a perfect attitude for dealing with conflict.

Exercise: What are your conflict skills?

Knowing our strengths and weaknesses in conflict is the beginning point for developing more confidence and skill in dealing with conflict. This exercise gives you an opportunity to think about the ways you approach conflict in your life. You may want to write down your answers to refer to as you continue reading the book.

1. How do you normally deal with conflicts in your life?

2. What are your strongest skills? What are your weak points? Make a list of these.
3. How would you describe your conflict style?

Thoughts to hold

- Women possess excellent conflict resolution skills: listening; empathy, care and concern; openness to learning; co-operation; verbal fluency; psychological flexibility; emotional honesty; self-reflection; intuition and insight; and practicality.
- Conflict skills can be difficult to use because they may be at odds with our beliefs about who we think we are or how we should be as women.
- Women and men tend to perceive and respond to conflict differently.
- Women tend to place a high value on relationship and cultivate skills that support emotional connection. Conflict can be seen as a threat to relationship.
- Fear of conflict is human and common but we can move beyond our fear.
- Conflict is an opportunity to learn something new about ourselves and others.
- Having a spiritual vision can empower us to deal with conflict.

2 Conflict – A Force of Nature

It isn't enough to talk about peace.
One must believe in it.
And it isn't enough to believe in it.
One must work at it.

Eleanor Roosevelt

Thomas Crumm, author of the classic conflict text *The Magic of Conflict*, writes that the action of the ocean crashing against the shore is nature in conflict – one force meeting another. Out of this natural event, shorelines are formed, creating splendour and beauty for all to behold and an abundance of tidal life with all its diverse wonders. That is conflict: the dynamic interaction of different forces which shape and change each other. Out of this dynamic interaction new life grows, transforming the old.

Transformation and change resulting from this dynamic interaction of opposites is an ancient idea found in Eastern spiritual philosophies such as Buddhism, Taoism and Hinduism, as well as Western psychological models such as Jungian, Gestalt and Process-oriented. With care and patience, it is possible to explore conflict and discover messages for change that will enrich and enhance our lives.

Crumm suggests that conflict is nature at work. Calling

conflict 'bad' is like calling the wind or rain or snow bad. Conflict just *is*. It is a naturally-occurring phenomenon that appears cyclically in the lives of individuals and societies. We could hardly grow without it. The types of conflicts that occur tell us a lot about the kind of life we lead and the kind of society we live in. So when you find yourself entangled in a conflict with someone, instead of thinking, 'This is bad', try thinking, 'This is nature and I'm part of it. How awesome'. And then ask yourself, 'What can I learn here? How can I settle this tension of opposites in a way that doesn't harm, but encourages learning and progress?'

What is conflict?

We may enjoy the poetic metaphor of conflict as the ocean crashing on a rocky shore, but what is it *really*? The answer is surprisingly simple: *conflict is tension.*

Tension is an everyday phenomenon that occurs whenever there is an obstacle or problematic difference between ourselves and another, or between two or more parts of ourselves. This tension can make us feel troubled, uncomfortable, insecure, afraid, irritated, excited or even hostile.

Tension is palpable and mood altering. As adrenaline pumps into our bloodstream we may feel tight or restless, our breathing may get shallower or faster, our stomach knotted or our teeth on edge. We are wired for fight or flight. Some people seem to thrive on this pumped up, living-on-the-edge feeling, but most of us like to avoid it as much as possible. In fact, our aversion to tension is so great that we go out of our way to avoid contact with people or topics that make us uncomfortable. We try to maintain tension-free lives. After all, who needs it? It is upsetting and tiring. The problem is, tension cannot be entirely avoided, especially in relationships with partners, colleagues, family and friends. Since some tension is inevitable, we need to learn how to deal with it.

But let's get even more basic: what *is* tension exactly, besides being an unpleasant sensation we would rather avoid? *Tension is concentrated energy.*

Tension is energy caught in a knot. Just like tension in your shoulders, the tension of conflict can feel hard and tight. This is why we feel relieved whenever we finally address a conflict, especially when we do it effectively. It clears the air and releases that knot of energy so we don't have to hold it anymore. Relief!

When we find ourselves in a conflict we are, in effect, polarised against another person. They think one thing and we think another. They want one thing and we want another. They see one thing and we see another. They say one thing and we say another, and so we ping-pong back and forth across the field of tension.

Conflicts are differences that polarise people and create tension.

We can't eliminate the presence of all tension from our lives, but the good news is that we can relieve many tensions through conflict resolution and use this energy for constructive purposes, such as to strengthen and deepen relationships and solve problems. When it comes to tension and conflict, we can either 'use it or be used by it'.

So, conflict resolution can be defined as *managing and reducing tension*.

By addressing and resolving tensions, we restore relationships, improve the atmosphere and find creative ways to get our needs met. After all, that is why tension is there in the first place – to alert us to a problem or a need for change.

In relationships we care about, tension is an indicator that something requires attention. It is a symptom. If it persists, we need to find out what is causing it and deal with it. Here are some negative and positive ideas about conflict. You can add your own ideas to the list.

Negative ideas of conflict

- Conflict is bad.
- Conflict means I have done something wrong.
- Conflict means the relationship is no good.
- Conflict means we are not meant to be together.
- Conflict means we don't love each other.
- Conflict means I can't have what I want.
- Conflict means I have failed.
- Conflict ruins everything – it destroys relationships.
- Conflict is what 'nice girls' don't do.

Positive ideas of conflict

- Conflict is part of the natural flow of life.
- Conflict is tension between two or more sides.
- Conflict is a knot of energy wrapped around a particular issue.
- Conflict is meaningful and has a purpose.
- Conflict is a signal that change is trying to happen.
- Conflict challenges us to grow and learn about ourselves and others.

- Conflict is an opportunity to create better relationships.
- Conflict helps create a more just world.
- Conflict adds creative challenge to life.

Symptoms of suppressed conflict

We all experience tension as a result of unresolved conflict in our lives. We feel these tensions in our bodies, in our relationships and in the emotional atmospheres of work and home. These tensions, when not addressed, can lead to a host of problems such as breakdown of relationships; feelings of low self-esteem, hopelessness and depression; physical symptoms; substance addictions; chronic unhappiness with home and work life; and a sense of meaninglessness and resignation.

When we are unable to deal with conflict, we often sacrifice our integrity by resorting to ineffective coping strategies. Resorting to these ineffective strategies reinforces our sense of powerlessness and fear.

Perhaps one of the most significant benefits of knowing how to deal with conflict is that we are empowered to maintain our true selves, even in the face of uncomfortable or stressful differences. Women who have learned to resolve conflict report a strengthened sense of self, improved atmosphere at home and work and a sense of hope (even excitement!) about their relationships and their lives. What is more, once you learn the simple tools of conflict resolution you have them for life – they are entirely portable!

Here are some symptoms of living in an atmosphere in which conflict is suppressed:

- avoiding people

- destructive gossip
- deadness or strain in relationships
- fear and anxiety
- fantasies of revenge or escape
- lack of intimacy or connection
- hopelessness, indifference and passivity
- complaining and blaming
- loss of focus and productivity
- sabotage of projects or events
- physical illness

Benefits of conflict resolution

These are some of the positive benefits of addressing conflict.
It takes time and effort but look at the results:

- tension reduction
- restored hope
- learning and growth
- renewed sense of relationship
- improved communication and intimacy
- interest and excitement
- realness and authenticity
- getting your needs met
- relief of stress and strain
- healthier atmosphere at home and work
- optimism about life and the future
- an opportunity to be influential
- increased freedom to be yourself
- solutions to problems
- directions for change

The conflict system

Let's take a simple example of conflict to illustrate our conflict resolution approach and see what it looks like in action. This example is of a small spat between intimate partners, Kate and Mark.

Kate and Mark have lived together for three years and get along well most of the time. Occasionally, they have small conflicts like the following one:

Kate shows Mark an article she is writing for work. She asks him what he thinks of it. Mark makes a few recommendations he thinks might improve her article. He feels he is being helpful. Kate becomes upset and says to Mark, 'You're always so critical. Why can't you say something positive?' Mark feels attacked and responds by saying, 'You ask me what I think but when I tell you, you don't like it! It's never the right thing for you, never good enough!'

Kate and Mark both feel criticised but neither thinks of themselves as being critical. This is a typical scenario of two people in conflict: two victims of criticism but no apparent critic. No one wants to take responsibility for being critical. No one wants to give in to the other side. Neither side can see or hear the other. Both sides simply want to defend their point of view.

Feel familiar? Most conflicts start with this basic pattern:
- feeling criticised, accused, misunderstood, hurt or threatened
- refusing to listen to the other side
- denying our own contribution to the problem
- wanting to 'save face'
- wanting to win

This is the initial stage of conflict – polarisation. It feels tense! So what should Kate and Mark do? Is Mark critical or is Kate insecure? How should they proceed?

Her side/his side

Let's proceed with the conflict by introducing our conflict resolution model. First, as in every conflict, there are two sides: Kate's Side and Mark's Side. There is also a knot of tension between them over a specific issue. Normally it takes a little time and discussion to identity what the central issue is. In this case, we might say that the central issue appears to be about criticism. Here's how it looks so far:

Kate's Side   **Mark's Side**

'You're critical and not   *'It's never good enough*
supportive!'   *for you!'*

Here's another way of looking at it:

Let's return now to Kate and Mark's conflict.

Both sides are looking tense and unhappy. Kate takes her side again. She repeats: 'Mark, you're so critical and negative.' Mark feels attacked again and says: 'I never can get it right with you, Kate, no matter how hard I try!' Kate and Mark are doing what everyone does: *they repeat their side even though that tactic isn't working.* Kate and Mark go back and forth, ping-ponging and getting nowhere fast. What's wrong here? First of all, both Kate and Mark are rigidly glued to their own side. How about introducing another viewpoint? Let's call this new viewpoint the neutral side.

Neutral Side

Kate accuses Mark of being critical. Mark accuses Kate of never being satisfied.
Both feel criticised. How can they resolve the conflict?
What's happening here?

Kate's Side	Mark's Side
'You're critical and not supportive!'	*'It's never good enough for you!'*

We can also look at it like this:

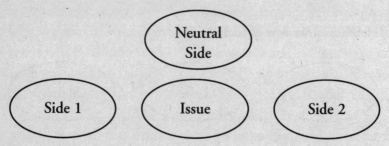

Now what?

Kate has an idea. She steps away from her own position and looks at the situation from a more neutral viewpoint. She notices a few things:

- neither one of them is listening to each other
- both of them are irritated and upset
- the conflict is escalating

- the central issue has not been truly identified. In other words, what are they fighting about? Do they know yet?

Kate decides on a new strategy: listening! She decides to listen to Mark to find out about his side. She says, 'Okay, Mark, tell me more about your side. I really want to understand it.' Kate takes Mark's side.

Mark is surprised by her sudden interest in his side. This is different, he thinks. He tells Kate that she's often unhappy with him, even when he tries to give her what she wants. For example, he genuinely felt the article could be improved by the suggestions he offered. It wasn't meant as a criticism but as constructive feedback. Kate considers what he has said. She asks one more question of Mark: what does he need in order to resolve this conflict?

Mark says he needs several things. He needs Kate to stop thinking he is being critical of her all the time. But more importantly, he needs Kate to ask for what she wants. If she wants positive feedback for her article, then ask for it. If she wants positive feedback *and* suggestions for improvement, ask for it. He doesn't like Kate's indirect way of asking for what she wants.

Mark's side is hard for Kate to hear. After all, who likes to admit their contribution to a problem? Kate, however, appreciates Mark's honesty and agrees that she doesn't always ask for what she wants. She doesn't want to blame him for that.

Mark is relieved that Kate is listening to him and owning her side of the problem. At this point, she's done a good job of taking his side. Emotions have begun to settle. Impressed by her ability to listen, Mark decides to return the favour and asks Kate what she needs from him.

Kate now takes her own side again. The problem she has with Mark is his lack of compliments. She feels he expresses his criticisms more readily than his praise. She wants Mark to be more positive. She can accept his criticisms when he also says what he likes. She wants more praise from him!

Mark considers this. His first impulse is to deny it. He praises her all the time! Or does he? He realises he feels the same way with his father, who's always telling Mark how to do better with his business. Mark is uncomfortable with this insight but says to Kate that he *can* be a bit on the negative side and forget to be positive. He certainly has lots of positive feelings for Kate! Kate smiles. The atmosphere has changed from hostility to honesty, from tension to greater relaxation. The work of conflict resolution has begun.

Let's look at some of the skills Kate and Mark used to reduce tension between them and deal with the issue at hand.

1. They used one of the fundamentals of conflict resolution: *keep it simple and specific.*

   There's no need for any lengthy analysis or long-winded confessions, or sharing of insights about your childhood, unless it's relevant or helps the conflict resolve. If you can stay with the specific conflict *in the moment* and resolve it simply and specifically, then do so. It really can be that simple at times.

2. They both *admitted to their contribution to the issue.*

Let's continue with our story of Kate and Mark.

In completing the conflict, Kate decides to take the neutral side again and offers an overview of the conflict. She says it seems that both of them want to be more appreciated and less criticised for what they do. Mark agrees with this. They both also agree that it feels good to be listening to each other and to be honest about what they want from each other. Kate and Mark walk into the kitchen to cook dinner. They don't discuss the conflict over dinner but enjoy the softer energy of making-up.

Most conflicts don't resolve as quickly or as smoothly as this model scenario, but many of them start as suddenly and as unexpectedly! Now let's look at a more detailed, step-by-step description of the skills of resolution.

The path to resolution

A resolution will emerge if both sides are able to express their viewpoint fully, listen carefully and learn about the other side. Resolution happens as a result of this process. When we truly listen to each other and express ourselves honestly, we discover new information about ourselves and about the issue at hand. This new information helps us resolve the conflict.

We can think of conflict as a system that holds three different positions within it. As we have seen in Kate and Mark's case, the first two positions in any conflict will be:

- Your Side
- The Other Side

We could also call this Side 1 and Side 2.

There is also a third position:

- The Neutral Side

When we think of conflict as a system with different positions, we develop an *overview of the process*. We are not merely swamped by our emotions. For instance, at the start of the argument Kate and Mark were absorbed in the hurt and angry feelings of their own side, but they had the potential to look at the conflict from a more neutral and objective position. Kate did this when she stepped away from her own side, listened to Mark and began viewing things from a more balanced perspective.

Approaching conflict in this way relieves us of the burden of having to find an immediate solution to the issue (what shall we do, who should change, who is right?) and places the focus on how we are reacting and responding to each other. Are we fighting fair? Are we listening to each other? Is someone dominating or just out to win? Are we open to learning? What needs to happen to resolve this conflict? This ability to step away from our side for a moment and look at what is happening more objectively is the magic key. In other words, it's important to respond, not merely react.

Let's now break down the different parts of a conflict shown in Kate and Mark's argument:

The issue is what is being discussed, such as money, time, work, power, housework, children, sex, relatives, support or criticism. In Kate and Mark's conflict the issue was criticism and appreciation.

The process is how the issue is being discussed. Is it fair, productive, honest and direct? Is it stuck somewhere? How are both people handling it? Initially, Kate and Mark handled the conflict by each taking their own side. This was a good beginning but it only was when they took each other's side that resolution became possible.

Personal/emotional conflicts are conflicts that enter the personal realm and become emotional in nature. Any conflict has the potential to become personal, depending on how important the issue is to us and how we treat each other during the discussion. Kate and Mark's conflict was highly personal and emotional. It was all about how they related to each other.

Impersonal/rational conflicts are problems that involve discussing options and making a decision on the best course of action. In these conflicts it is possible to stay focused on the issue at hand and not become emotionally involved. Workplace conflicts are often of this nature but too often become personal and emotional when people use poor conflict resolution skills. Kate and Mark's argument started over Kate's article but soon escalated into a more personal issue between them.

The three steps of conflict resolution

The three key positions (your side, other side, and neutral side) give rise to the three steps of conflict resolution:
1. Take Your Own Side
2. Take the Other Side
3. Take the Neutral Side

Each of these steps uses a different skill. The skills needed for each step are:
1. Speak your needs and wants (take your own side)
2. Listen and learn (take the other side)
3. Look objectively at what is happening (take the neutral side)

I sometimes shorten this to *Speak, Listen and Look*. Each of these steps is addressed in the next three chapters. I have broken down the procedure into three distinct steps so that you can become familiar with the process. In an actual conflict, you would move through all three steps fluidly, as you felt the need, as many times as is necessary to resolve it. Conflict is resolved best when we feel free to move back and forth between the various viewpoints and not be glued rigidly to our own side.

When we learn to drive a car we break it down into parts and learn about each part, such as the accelerator pedal, the brakes and steering wheel. Once we are actually driving, we move fluidly back and forth between the separate pedals and wheel in a smooth flow of action. In our conflict resolution model, we might say that taking our own side is like using the accelerator, pressing forward with our viewpoint. Taking the other side is like using the brakes, slowing down or stopping for others. Taking the neutral side is like using the steering wheel as we wisely guide the process, keeping an eye on where we are and where we want to go.

By using these three unique perspectives – your side, the other side and the neutral side – we gain the information we need to resolve our conflicts in a fair and friendly manner.

The key is within you

The solutions to your conflicts are *within you*. We each possess within us the resources and wisdom to solve our conflicts and find new conflict-free directions for living. We may need support at times to discover the answers, but the answers are available within us if we give ourselves an opportunity to explore.

One of the most important keys to resolving conflict is taking a neutral or objective perspective. While there is no perfect neutrality or objectivity in life, the Neutral Side is simply the capacity to maintain an overview in order to help each side communicate effectively and fairly. In third-party mediation, a mediator, manager or counsellor occupies this neutral role. Parents occupy this role with squabbling siblings. However, we can learn to occupy this role in our own conflicts. It simply requires the ability to step aside for a few minutes and assess the situation as a whole. You can learn to referee your own conflicts. Kate stepped into the Neutral Side during her conflict with Mark when she first noticed that neither of them was listening to each other. That was a helpful observation.

The Neutral Side is a non-partisan viewpoint that supports both sides to work it out together. It wants the relationship itself to win. This balanced viewpoint is easier said than done when you're in the middle of a heated fight with someone!

Why does conflict happen so frequently in life? One reason is that we are all growing and changing and bumping into other growing and changing beings. This is challenging for us all. Another reason is that we lack conflict resolution skills, so the same old conflicts keep cycling endlessly, creating a sense of anger and hopelessness. Sometimes it takes repeating a conflict many times before we 'get it'. The good news is that even when practical solutions are slow in coming, the *spirit* of relationship is nourished when tensions are acknowledged and brought out into the open.

Story: The link between inner and outer conflict

Amanda is an attractive thirty-year-old woman who was thinking of ending her five-year marriage. Bit by bit, she'd closed down emotionally. I asked her what made her most angry with her husband. She told me he had a bad habit of spacing out and not listening when she spoke. She thought he might even have attention deficient disorder. He himself admitted he had trouble tuning into people when they spoke. Amanda wanted to forgive him but felt too frustrated and angry.

First of all I did some inner conflict resolution work with Amanda. I asked her about the two different sides of herself: the one that wanted to leave the marriage and the one that wanted to stay. Amanda said that she saw two little figures sitting on each shoulder, one saying she expected too much in relationship and the other saying she expected too little. I asked her which side she usually listened to. She said the voice that told her she expected too much. This side tolerated her husband's 'deafness' and felt sorry for him. After all, this was a behaviour he seemed unable to change.

Amanda had just about used up all her tolerance and compassion. She was furious and burned-out. Unconditional love had not worked. I asked her how she might be different if she listened to the other voice, the one that said she expected too little. She said, 'Well, I don't want to be a General!' I suggested that by not listening to this less tolerant part of herself, she had allowed the frustration to build up to the point where she was about to give her husband his marching orders. She was indeed about to become a General.

Amanda's story shows us how her inner and outer conflict were linked; her inner dilemma about whether she should have high or low expectations of relationship had led to an uneasy tolerance of her husband's behaviour. When we deny important parts of ourselves, they eventually come up for reckoning.

Likewise, when we deny tensions in our relationships for too long, they can suddenly explode with destructive results.

Amanda needed to resolve her inner conflict about her expectations in relationship before she could address her outer conflict with her husband over not being heard. No one had been listening to Amanda – neither herself, nor her husband. That had to change.

When Amanda resolved her inner conflict by deciding that being heard was a realistic expectation in relationship, it shook up the marriage. As her husband, Peter, heard the seriousness of her complaint, he became eager to resolve the conflict and save the marriage. They began couples counselling. Peter agreed to be assessed for attention deficient disorder. As there was a deep love between them, they had a good chance of resolving their differences and creating a stronger marriage.

Moral of the story: Listen to yourself first

This story demonstrates the importance of taking your own side. If Amanda had continued to deny her feelings, her resentment might have built up to the point where resolution was difficult to achieve. Amanda's story also shows us how our inner conflicts can block us from dealing with our tensions with others. In Amanda's case, her identity as a woman included telling herself not to expect more from a relationship, despite the inner tension that created in her! She told herself she must be more accepting and non-demanding. This limiting belief made it difficult for her to address her problem with Peter head on. She had learned two vital lessons about conflict resolution: *our beliefs can hinder us in dealing with conflict*, and *if we want others to listen to us, we must listen to ourselves first.*

We'll explore beliefs that hinder or help in the next chapter.

Just as in Amanda's story, the daily tensions we experience inside ourselves and with others act as magnets, drawing us to those issues that require attention. By avoiding tensions we get ourselves into some pretty big messes. As we learn to deal with our conflicts, they become less dramatic and more satisfying. We conflict less often, less harshly and more productively. That's because we get better at resolving conflicts as they occur. We get clearer about what we want. We get smarter about which tensions to tackle and which to leave to dissolve on their own. We commit to building more peaceful and nurturing lives. We take greater responsibility for ourselves and blame others less. Every good partnership, whether personal or professional, involves understanding the keys of conflict resolution.

In the next chapter we look at the first step in this process: how you can take your own side more effectively in conflict.

Exercise: Tension-spotting

Noticing and acknowledging tension is the first step to building a peaceful life. This exercise shows you how to spot the tensions in your life. You may want to write your answers down for future reference.

1. Where do you feel tension in your life?
2. With whom do you feel tension in your life?
3. What is the cost of this tension on your health and happiness?
4. Where do you feel at peace in your life?
5. With whom do you feel at peace in your life?

6. Make a list of the tension spots you would like to resolve in your life.

Thoughts to hold

- Conflict is tension. Tension is concentrated energy that can be used productively.
- Conflict resolution is tension management and reduction.
- A conflict has three sides: your side, the other side and the neutral side.
- Taking Your Side requires the skill of speaking your needs and wants.
- Taking the Other Side requires the skill of listening and learning.
- Taking the Neutral Side requires the skill of looking objectively at what is happening.
- Conflict resolution skills can be simplified to: Speak, Listen and Look.

---

3 Take Your Own Side: The Big Breakthrough

Courage is the price life exacts for granting peace.

Amelia Earhart

The first and most fundamental element in conflict resolution is the ability and willingness of each party to take his or her side. That is, to speak. This means being able to state clearly, and defend if necessary, your viewpoint on whatever issue is causing tension. Without this, there is little chance for a satisfactory resolution. No conflict can be truly resolved unless both sides are represented. If you want to resolve a conflict, you have to take your own side. This is the most important step. No amount of apologising, forgiving or understanding can make up for the fact you haven't expressed your side.

Only after you've put all the information on the table does real discussion occur. Only then does the magic of conflict resolution reveal itself. 'You mean I can't resolve conflict by being nice only?' In a word, no. Taking risks and staying committed to the conversation is the way to resolve conflict.

Resolution is about connection

Conflict can be scary, but at its core, conflict resolution is about connection, not separation. Without doing our part by taking our own side, we cannot resolve conflict. We can avoid conflict, we can deny it and we can resist it. But ultimately, to resolve it, we need to participate.

Conflict resolution is not only about taking our side, it is about reconciling our differences through the process of conversation: speaking, listening, learning, seeing and connecting. At its core, conflict resolution is about *connection*, which is why so many women are interested in conflict resolution today – women believe in the value and importance of connection between people. The good news is conflict resolution allows you to take your own side in a way that doesn't jeopardise your relationships but strengthens them.

Story: Getting workplace respect

In this story we look at conflict in a workplace environment, often the most difficult place to resolve tensions and take one's own side.

Nandini was a nurse manager in a hospital where, sadly, it was not uncommon for a certain doctor to talk down to nurses. Normally Nandini accepted this behaviour with good humour and tolerance. She saw it as one of the unavoidable stresses of the job – it came with the territory, so to speak. But this attitude was about to change.

One day the doctor was displeased with a management decision she'd made. He turned to a colleague and swore colourfully about Nandini in front of her and other staff. She felt shamed and put-down by this public disrespect. This behaviour was overstepping the line even for good-natured Nandini.

Nandini came to see me because she didn't want to be treated like this but was afraid to approach the doctor in question. She needed support to take her own side. Nandini had taken an important first step: *knowing when to get help to take your own side*.

I coached Nandini by asking her to identify the key issue, as she saw it. The key issue for her was respect. The second was that she wanted to maintain a good relationship with the doctor. Third, she felt it was important for her as a manager not to accept this behaviour. After all, if she accepted it, what message did that send to young nurses on her staff?

I cautioned Nandini that the doctor would probably feel threatened by her raising the issue and might attempt to divert the conversation away from *his* behaviour and toward the management decision *she'd* made. She was to calmly but surely keep the conversation on the key issue – his disrespectful manner of communicating about her in public. Nandini was now engaged in another important step: *planning your approach and for any likely reactions*.

Finally, I asked Nandini what she wanted from the doctor. She wanted an apology and to be treated with respect. This is key for taking your own side: *knowing what you want to get out of a conflict*.

So, how did Nandini's story end? Nandini approached the doctor in his office the very next day. She remained calm and clear and practised the hardest and most important skill in conflict resolution: *emotional discipline*. In other words, she kept her cool.

Nandini chose to build rapport with the doctor first by commenting that they'd both been in the industry for a long time and had worked together for many years. She then told him that his swearing about her in public had hurt her feelings and was disrespectful. The doctor, as predicted, attempted to divert the conversation. Nandini calmly brought it back to the issue of his behaviour. To his credit, he wisely saw that the game was up, offered an apology and promised it wouldn't happen again. After all, who could argue with such a clear and forthright request? They agreed to treat each other with respect and parted on friendly terms.

Once back in her own office, Nandini whooped for joy and then phoned to tell me of her success. What a great feeling to speak up for one's side and be heard! Her nurses heard the story and were inspired. Nandini had taken powerful action to help change the traditional hospital culture between doctors and nurses – a small step of great significance. Nandini got what she wanted without losing it.

Resolving tensions through conversation

How did Nandini achieve her simple but stunning success? She did it through the power of conversation. And by carefully and courageously taking her own side.

If you think you're being helpful by denying your own viewpoint, you're probably not. It's more likely that you're blocking the possibility of resolution. After all, you can't resolve conflict by avoiding it. Remaining silent may be appropriate in certain emergency or survival situations, but it doesn't work well as a strategy for your daily on-going relationships. Taking your own side and being clear about your needs is your best bet for health and happiness at work and at home.

To take our own side, we need a voice. Without a voice, it's difficult to resolve differences in our relationships. We simply give in. Sometimes finding our voice during conflict can be difficult, so we'll explore ways to find our voice later in this chapter. By using our voice, we claim the freedom to take our own side.

What stops women from taking their own side?

There are a number of reasons why a woman might have trouble taking her own side. Knowing what gets in our way allows us to take appropriate steps to overcome these barriers and move forward.

Old gender roles

Despite great strides made by women in the areas of work, education and equal opportunity, traditional social roles are not altogether gone. Many women have been conditioned by culture – by mothers as well as mates – to believe that a woman's opinion isn't as important as a man's, or that her feelings are irrelevant. This message is partly rooted in a society that places more value on the intellectual and less on the emotional or intuitive aspects of consciousness. We have been told our feelings and opinions don't count, are not interesting, or beside the point, so we tell ourselves that our gut reactions are not important or relevant and that it is better to hold our peace. The belief has become internalised. An inner voice repeatedly tells us to keep our mouth shut, play it safe, and that our role is to understand and support others. We feel we 'ask too much' when we want others to listen to and understand us. This sense of unworthiness can hold us back from taking our own side. US self-help exponent Oprah Winfrey has called this the 'disease to please'.

While these social messages and patterns are changing, it's a slow process.

Gender roles are changing

But gender roles are changing, and with this change come new possibilities for equality and fluidity in communication. For a relationship to be sustainable, there must be a certain degree of equality and symmetry in communication and in the way we conflict. Both sides must be represented, without the submission of either. When someone feels they must continually surrender their side, they may eventually express their side by exploding, leaving the relationship, resigning their job, under-performing at work, lodging complaints, having affairs, developing physical symptoms, getting depressed, turning off sexually, or seeking justice or revenge in some other way. When each side is supported to express itself fully, unexpected options for resolution emerge. The new equality developing between men and women in relationships and in the workplace bodes well for all of us to resolve our differences with respect and acceptance.

Family rules learned in childhood

Another obstacle to taking our own side is the pattern we learned from our parents and caretakers for handling conflict. Every family has its own rules for handling conflict. Some families forbid conflict and discourage children for speaking up or expressing themselves. Other families are full of strife but never manage to resolve their tensions. Other families are polite and avoid discussing difficult topics. Some families have different rules for male and female children. The lessons we learned in childhood about conflict often accompany us for the rest of our lives.

Many women learned as young girls that it was not safe to disagree with men. Girls who are told they were stupid or selfish can have trouble in later life speaking up, defending themselves or asking for what they want. As a result of these experiences, they fear conflict situations, where they experience in a painful way their difficulty in disagreeing or holding an argument. Becoming aware of our family patterns is a powerful step toward freeing ourselves of habits that no longer serve us. Once we know the patterns that hold us back, we can learn to deal with conflict successfully.

What are some patterns you learned as a child?

Women's relationship orientation

While some women may have trouble taking their own side, they're often very skilled at taking the other side: listening, building bridges and nurturing relationship. Women's general tendency to foster connection and relationship is a great strength but it can also lead to a weakness in conflict: fearing and avoiding conflict because it appears to threaten what is held most dear – emotional connection with others. This tendency can impel women to cling to the sense of connection at all costs, even when it's bad for their mental and emotional health to do so.

Some women have confided to me that they feel so much pressure to look after others that breaking this implicit social contract, by voicing their own needs, throws them into a panic. They feel that expressing their needs will ruin everything. These women crave harmony and security and cannot tolerate the tension created by speaking up. However, respectfully sharing your viewpoint and gently but firmly holding to it until you feel heard has an empowering effect on your life. It also has a cleansing and balancing effect on your relationships.

Men and women argue differently

As Deborah Tannen, author of *You Just Don't Understand*, has pointed out, men and women use different rules for conversation. It's true that they also employ similar rules but the differences are worth noting. As mentioned in Chapter 1, Deborah Tannen calls these differences Report Talk and Rapport Talk. When men talk, they tend to give a report of the information they want to get across. When women talk, they tend to establish rapport with the other person by finding commonalties, taking turns at talking and asking questions. They are more interested in establishing connection than in providing information – rapport talk.

The same is often true of conflict. Men and women argue differently at times. A man may come to the table with his position already established. He may have discovered his position through thinking it out on his own. A woman may come to the table expecting to have a conversation that will allow her to discover her side. She may feel confronted by the fact that the man already knows what he thinks and doesn't appear to be interested in helping her discover her side. If the man thinks the woman needs help discovering her side, he may, as John Gray puts it, try to 'fix' her, by encouraging her to take a position that isn't right for her. Often, the woman doesn't want to be fixed but to be listened to until she has explored her thoughts and feelings to her satisfaction. Alternately, the man may take advantage of her uncertainty by pushing his agenda ahead of hers. She may give in to his agenda because she feels insecure about not having a firm position ready to debate.

Women discover their side through relating and conversing

Women often discover their side through talking. We go to therapists in droves just to get this vital need met – to discover our own needs and feelings.

Trying to talk with a male partner before discovering one's side can put women at a disadvantage. Traditionally, women have always consulted with each other before and after any major event in their lives, including tensions with their partners. This behaviour has often been seen as gossiping, but in reality it provides a very important function. It allows women to discover and affirm their feelings and needs through talking with a supportive listener. It is the path of mutual discovery though relating and conversing. It is consulting.

A woman can feel frustrated when a man tries to fix her problems. She wants to be listened to supportively and allowed to make her own discoveries. Some men are gifted at providing this kind of listening support for a woman. In this case, both the man and woman can talk and listen in ways that nurture each other and allow for mutual discovery.

Simply recognising the different ways men and women conflict is helpful. You could call them the Individualist approach to conflict versus the Mutual Discovery approach. In fact, these two styles of taking one's own side may be found between any two people of either gender. It's important not to criticise people for how they approach conflict. Criticising and blaming only makes matters worse. What is needed is an examination and understanding of differing styles. Most people are willing to explore new behaviours when they feel supported and accepted. Most of us do not grow in circumstances of judgment or blame. Therefore we need to allow ourselves to explore new behaviours in ways that are respectful.

It's easy to blame others for not understanding us, for being insensitive, for dominating and not hearing us. It's easy to justify our own behaviour by citing that of our parents, bosses, partners or the opposite gender. But it's ultimately more rewarding to take responsibility for our own behaviour and for learning new behaviours.

Beliefs

Along with a tendency to disregard our own feelings, needs and perceptions, women may unconsciously believe that we have to 'lose' in order to keep our relationships. We give up our viewpoint in order not to risk losing our connection with another. We 'neutralise' conflicts by agreeing or apologising. In a way, this generous attitude does hold relationships together, and it certainly holds families together during times of stress. Women's ability to de-escalate conflict through their sensitivity, humility and emotional generosity is a true but little recognised skill. The danger, however, is that it may create a chronic communication pattern of 'giving in'. Always giving in can lead to pseudo intimacy and false harmony in relationship, as honest self-expression is blocked. It may even create a dominant–submissive pattern, whereby we surrender our viewpoint for the sake of continuity of relationship. In this way we collude with the inequality that has been part of the unspoken emotional contract between men and women.

These various beliefs are all interlinked in complex ways and can act together as a powerful force to hinder a woman from taking her own side. Alternatively, depending on how these and other factors have played out in our lives, we may have developed a deep inner well of confidence and unshakeable self-belief – all vital qualities for taking our own side successfully. What's important to remember is that it's never too late to develop robust self-respect and self-confidence, and it's never too late to learn how to take our own side effectively.

Story: Margot's beliefs

Your beliefs about yourself as a woman either help or hinder your ability to take your own side in a conflict. One evening in my conflict resolution class, an energetic and passionate woman named Margot was stymied when she tried practising taking her own side. She simply couldn't do it, even though she was frustrated with her husband's lack of interest in sexual contact and wanted to raise the issue with him. I asked Margot what belief she had about herself that might be holding her back from pursuing this conversation with her husband. After thinking for a moment, a light bulb went on in her head. Margot said she had always believed she shouldn't make others feel uncomfortable. She did not want him to feel bad.

This is a common belief for many. We believe we shouldn't make others uncomfortable or pressure them in any way. It's part of what is commonly known as the Terminal Niceness Syndrome. But to reduce tensions by negotiating effectively, we need to bring a certain degree of pressure to the table. Usually, despite our beliefs, people are not as fragile as they appear and often respond well to respectful challenge and debate. Keeping people comfortable doesn't necessarily resolve issues.

I coached Margot on the skills of taking her own side. I also asked her to create a new belief for herself that would support her to speak up with her husband, even if it created some discomfort for him initially. Margot's new belief was that it was okay for her to make others uncomfortable in order to resolve issues.

Margot gathered up her courage and approached her husband about the lack of passion in their relationship. It did make him uncomfortable at first, as she had feared, but it also brought them close together by opening up a deep and intimate conversation between them. Margot, inspired by her success, decided to approach her workplace manager to discuss her dissatisfaction with her job. Her manager was less receptive than her husband had been. The outcome of this conversation was that Margot decided to apply for – and won – a more rewarding and better-paid position. Margot learned that having the courage to face the discomfort of conflict often brings big rewards.

Ask your friends about their beliefs about conflict. It might prove enlightening! Recently I had some friends over to dinner, a lovely couple, Carla and Michael. I asked them about their conflict patterns. They both agreed they rarely conflicted openly. I asked them why not. Michael said, 'I don't want to blame. That's not productive.' Carla smiled mischievously and said, 'It all happens at the subterranean level.' Michael believed that conflict meant blaming the other, so naturally he wanted to avoid conflict. But Carla knew their resentments leaked out in other more subtle ways.

Over the years I have collected women's beliefs about conflict. Here are a few common examples:

- I shouldn't make others uncomfortable.
- I should accept others as they are.
- Conflict will ruin everything.
- He or she will get angry with me if I take my own side.
- I will hurt people's feelings and they won't like me.
- I don't want to blame others – it's not productive.
- It is not nice to argue.
- I will get hurt.
- I will lose control.
- It is dangerous to say what you think.

Women's beliefs about conflict can be organised into three main categories:

1. **If I take my own side, it will ruin the relationship:** This belief is about making others happy and keeping things safe so that the relationship will not be disturbed. Without your efforts to this end, the relationship will fall apart. It's based on the idea of the emotional fragility or selfishness of others – that is, that other people can't cope with your needs or who you really are. You have to keep others comfortable so they will not collapse, get hurt or withdraw their support.

Story: Nancy sees it through

Nancy had been recently promoted to head of the accounts department in an IT firm. The accounts department had a history of antagonism and mutual complaint with the technical department, supposedly due to the difficult personality of the head of that department, Susan, a forceful and somewhat aggressive woman. Soon after Nancy's promotion, Susan called, coolly congratulated her on her promotion and suggested they meet to discuss a list of complaints she'd received about accounts. When they met, Nancy saw that many of the complaints had merit. As Nancy was an excellent communicator and relationship builder, she calmly took Susan's side and sorted through each complaint in a professional and responsive manner. Susan appeared pleasantly surprised by Nancy's non-adversarial approach and left feeling confident her complaints would be resolved satisfactorily. When Nancy told her two middle managers how well the meeting had gone with the head of the technical department, they reacted with dismay: had Nancy advocated for accounts? What about *their* complaints? Had she capitulated to technical? Nancy felt her success begin to crumple. Did her managers have a point – had she let her department down?

After a quick analysis, it became clear what she needed to do. Nancy was very good at taking the other side. She was also quite good at taking the neutral side and maintaining her objectivity and perspective. These skills made her an excellent relationship builder. However, she needed to become stronger at taking her own side – her weak spot. The belief system that held this weak spot in place was that taking her own side would ruin her relationships. She didn't want to do anything that might seem demanding, confronting, accusing or pressurising. This was a belief system that needed changing! I helped Nancy come up with a new belief to transform her weak spot into a strength. Her new belief was that taking your own side gives others an opportunity to give back and do something positive for you.

I suggested that Nancy go back to Susan and continue the discussion. Nancy was afraid at first because she didn't want to upset the apple cart. She feared the old Accounts–Technical antagonism would be revived. However, a week later she contacted Susan and raised her department's complaints in a courteous manner, silently repeating to herself her new belief that this would give Susan an opportunity to give back and do something positive for her. To her relief, Susan received her concerns calmly and agreeably. Susan was a tough woman but not an unreasonable one. She appreciated Nancy's thoughtful and sincere style, so different from the last head of accounts! Nancy had just taken an enormous step in her leadership and conflict resolution skills.

2. **If I take my side, they'll get me for it:** This belief says that others are dangerous and vengeful and will seek retribution if you aren't what they want you to be. Like the first belief, it is fear-driven. Unfortunately, many women *have* experienced negative consequences when they took their own side, so this lends credibility to the belief. However, most often, this belief is based on conditioning learned in childhood, not on current circumstances. But if this belief keeps you from taking your own side, it can perpetuate the problem, like a self-fulfiling prophecy. If you are afraid of another's anger, it's not likely that you can participate effectively in the conflict resolution process.

Story: Alice's unexpressed anger

Alice consistently communicated her objections in a disjointed and vague fashion. This frustrated and confused her partner, who would then get angry, unwittingly expressing the very anger Alice could not express. Alice was convinced that if she expressed her anger, her partner would get even angrier with her. This was a case of the belief system *'If I take my side, they'll get me for it'*. This may have been true once when she was a child but now it had become a self-fulfilling prophecy. The moral of this story is that if you don't take your own side, someone will take it for you. And not in a way that necessarily advances your interests.

3. **I can't take my own side because I'm wrong to feel this way:** This insidious belief says that whatever you need, feel or perceive is *your* problem. You shouldn't bother others with it. Maybe if you just worked on yourself more, the problem would go away. This belief stems from a deep despair about ever being understood or supported. It comes from a feeling that your needs are wrong. You don't expect others to care deeply about you, so you don't even try to be understood.

   These beliefs interfere with our capacity to communicate effectively. But by becoming aware of these background beliefs we are able to make new choices about how we will behave.

   Take a moment to think about your own beliefs:
   • What are the beliefs that make it hard for you to take your own side?
   • Where did they come from?

Story: Jackie stands up for herself

Jackie applied for a job at a family counselling agency. After the initial interview, one of the recruiting officers on the selection panel advised Jackie of the next step in the selection process. She was curt and dismissive with Jackie, even rude. Jackie immediately felt she must have preformed badly in her interview. She even considered withdrawing from the selection process, ready to believe she wasn't good enough for the job. I told her to call the recruiting officer immediately and explain how concerned she was about the way the officer had spoken with her – especially given they were a counselling agency. In other words, I encouraged Jackie not to assume she had performed badly and to stand up for herself, a somewhat daring move in the midst of a selection process. But as I said to Jackie, did she really want to work for an agency that spoke to her like that?

Jackie called the officer and told her how she felt. The officer immediately apologised and blamed her poor behaviour on stress and time pressures. She'd been unaware of the impact of her communication and was truly sorry. Happily, Jackie was offered a position in the agency, which did not surprise me in the least. Later Jackie said to me, 'You were so on my side!'. Well naturally! Before you decide you've done something wrong, check it out with the other side.

Replace limiting beliefs with big bold expansive ones

If you suffer from beliefs that hold you back from taking your own side, create new positive beliefs. In the story 'Margot's beliefs', p. 46, Margot believed that she shouldn't make others uncomfortable. This paralysed her from approaching her husband about her unhappiness. By becoming aware of her old belief and seeing its paralysing effect upon her, Margot felt motivated to create a new belief for herself. She created a belief that acted as a powerful reminder of who she wanted to be, someone who was confident enough to push others out of their comfort zone.

Your new belief should be so powerful and compelling that it obliterates the old limiting belief. Once you have found your new belief, write it down where you can read it easily. Put it in your wallet, on your mirror, on the dashboard in your car or on your computer. Here are some examples of new beliefs women have created:

- I am clear and powerful in conflict.
- Telling my side frees me.
- I am an audacious and outspoken woman.
- Fear has no hold on me.
- My boldness brings opportunities into my life.
- The world needs me to express myself confidently.
  What belief do you want to create?

Intimidation tactics

Sometimes we don't take our own side because we're intimidated by the other person, whether man or woman. It's easy to become blocked from taking our own side if someone challenges us on every little point along the way. We can be kept permanently distracted from discovering or expressing our real needs if we are tied up in semantic debates and side issues.

We can also lose our ground when we're interacting with someone who uses dirty fighting tactics such as bullying or blaming. We react by retaliating or withdrawing. Many conflicts get stuck in a meaningless cycle of attack and revenge. This is definitely a phase of conflict – the phase of not listening. Conflict escalates when people feel blamed and not heard.

Recognise and be prepared for intimidation tactics

If you fear going into a discussion with an intimidating person, prepare yourself ahead of time – discover your side before going into the conflict. You can do this by talking first with a friend or colleague. Quiet reflection or meditation is also a great way to get clear about your side. Chapter 12 discusses Clean and Dirty Fighting and what you can do if you are confronted with an intimidating or dirty fighter. Don't feel pushed into a conflict you are not ready for. Buy time if you need to.

Buying time for your side

As we've seen, women more than men get clear about what they think and feel by talking with others. Much of the time we don't know where we stand on an issue until we articulate it. That is the value of conversation. A great deal of our self-knowledge is gleaned through the process of sharing our opinions, perceptions, feelings and needs with others. Sometimes it's not necessary to come to the negotiation table with a fully worked out position. We just need to start a conversation and keep it going long enough for both people to discover and express their sides.

Sometimes women say, 'But discovering my side takes time. What if I have to respond immediately?' Women also say they feel stupid during conflict – they feel pressured to respond but can't think of what to say until a day or week later. I advise women who have this problem to memorise a stock list of statements to use to buy time. You don't have to know your side completely; you just have to know you have one. Here is a sample list to use when you need time to discover your side.

- I disagree but I'm not yet sure why.
- I need time to think about this. I'll follow up on this later.
- This doesn't feel right to me for some reason.
- I have different feelings about that, some of which are not yet fully formed.
- I am surprised by what you said. I need a moment to think about it.
- Give me a moment to think. I'll respond in a minute.
- Please say more about your side. I need to hear more about this.
- May I explore another viewpoint?
- Let's make a time to talk about this later.
- I need to come back to this.

These stock statements give you a few seconds to gather yourself, while letting the other side know you have your own viewpoint and are not merely agreeing. Making a general statement of disagreement can get you over the hurdle of taking your own side. Just stating that you have another perspective is the first step and puts you in line for the next step – finding out what it is.

How to take your own side

Now that we have explored some of the barriers to taking your own side, how do you actually do it? Each of the three steps of conflict resolution – taking your side, taking the other side and taking the neutral side – requires a different skill. The first skill of taking your side requires using our power to assert our viewpoint and express our needs.

Taking your own side is often experienced energetically as pushing or moving forward. Asserting yourself is like putting your foot on the accelerator. Here are the skills you need to take your own side:

- exploring what you think, feel, need or want
- believing in yourself
- asking for what you want
- being vulnerable and self-disclosing
- finding the courage to express your viewpoint, even if risky or unpopular
- having the patience to allow others to learn and understand your side
- disagreeing respectfully
- willingness to 'hang in there' and not give up
- resisting pressure or bullying
- providing specific details
- knowing and being clear about your limits
- practising honesty and constructive criticism

Having a voice

Using your voice is how you represent yourself to others and make yourself heard. This ability comes from believing in yourself and your right to be who you are. It comes from seeing that your needs are important, even if different from others. It comes from seeing yourself as a woman who is participating in the democratic system of free speech and debate.

Discovering what you want

In conflict, we need to discover our side. Discovery is the process of uncovering something that is invisible or not yet known. As discussed earlier, men and women tend to deal with conflict differently. One difference I have observed is that women tend to discover their side through mutual conversation, men by thinking about it alone. This difference can disadvantage a woman in a conflict with a man. The woman will want to talk about the issue to discover their viewpoint. The man may come to the table with their position already established. From the perspective of the man, the woman looks weak by not having her position already in place. She may find herself being pushed around by the man's position. The man's already established position can override the woman's need for conversation and mutual discovery. Knowing this, a woman can ask the man to listen to her while she finds her position. Better still, she can talk with a friend to get clear on her position beforehand. Preparation helps you to feel confident and clear.

With practice we can get quicker and more skilful at taking our own side. We sense when we are holding back what we really think, feel and want. We get better at taking risks and standing up for ourselves. We get better at trusting our perceptions and voicing them. Often we know our own side of a conflict, but we hold back for fear of saying the wrong thing or going 'too far'. We have so much conditioning and fear that we override our true perceptions and wants.

Your feelings are keys

What are feelings? Feelings are our gut-level responses, our naked self. A feeling is the most personal detail about you. That is why we often feel vulnerable about revealing them. We all have ideas but they're not necessarily intimate or personal. When, how and why you have feelings is unique to you and others come to know you intimately through the revelation of them. I once had a wonderful mentor who often stopped me when I talked abstractly about myself. I resented him when he did this but he would only laugh and say, 'You hate it when I make you talk from your guts!' Indeed I did but I knew he was right.

Feelings are the glue that holds relationships together. They can be positive or negative, hidden or revealed, abusive or respectful. Even business relationships are based on goodwill and positive feelings. A company's success is often determined by the feelings of its consumers.

Often, just expressing our feelings is enough to get us where we want to go – peaceful resolution. Expressing our feelings bypasses the intellectualisations and rationalisations that can keep a conflict stuck. Feelings get straight to the point – our needs and wants.

It has often been more acceptable for women to express their feelings than men. This can give a woman a clear advantage in conflict. She can know and name her feelings faster than a man. This helps her identify the key issues on her side. Many men feel awkward and ill at ease when communication becomes personal and feeling-oriented, since discussion of feelings has often been seen as a traditionally female process. Feelings are seen as belonging to the irrational and unproductive realm of femininity. This is gradually changing as both men and women become adept at communicating their feelings, as well as their ideas.

Despite the permission granted to women to express their

feelings, many people, men and women alike, are unsure of their feelings and balk at revealing them. In many families we were taught to stuff our feelings down. Anger is a particularly challenging emotion for many women to express because anger often threatens the harmonious fabric of social connection. For many men it is the opposite; they balk at revealing vulnerability or fear because it threatens a masculine identity based on being strong. Many times I have worked with a couple and watched the woman express her deepest feelings while the man sits there looking embarrassed. But sometimes it's the woman who has trouble knowing her feelings.

How do you *feel* feelings? One way is to tune into your body. What is happening in your body? Are your teeth clenched? Is your heart beating fast? Are you slumped in resignation? Are you yelling inside your head? Being aware of what's happening in your body helps you discover your side and moves you closer to expressing it. We will talk more about the body's role in conflict in Chapter 7, Nonverbal Communication.

Exercise: Quick guide to using your feelings during conflict

1. Think of a tension or conflict you have with someone.
2. Now scan your body and notice what feelings are there. What do you feel exactly when you think of the tension with this person? Give these feelings a name.
3. Do you feel this often in relation to this person or situation? Check to see if there are other feelings lurking in the background you'd prefer to hide. Include these too.
4. If your feelings could speak, what would they say about what you need in the situation?

5. Imagine sharing your feelings with this person and telling them what you need. You are now clear about your side.
6. Scan yourself again. Have your feelings changed at all, even in a small way?

What do women want?

The answer to that one is easy. Most people want more or less of something in their lives. More time, less stress, more money, less pressure, more romance, less work, more sex, less sex, more power, less dependence, more social life, less loneliness, more recognition, less blame, more space, less competition, more appreciation, less criticism, more love, less pain. Whatever you want more or less of at any moment is your side. Accept it.

- Name three things you want more of in your life.
- Name three things you want less of in your life.

Using your self awareness

Resolving tensions with others requires having an awareness of what is happening within you. What are you feeling and thinking? How are you behaving? It also requires an awareness of what is happening with your conflict partner. How do they look? Is he or she listening or withdrawing? How are they behaving?

One of the things I notice with people in conflict is how little awareness they have about what is happening between them. Often people don't seem to register the other side's look of fear or hurt, nor do they hear their own condescending voice tone. And they usually miss the moment their conflict partner apologises. When we become emotional or tense, our awareness of ourselves and others often diminishes.

Not only do most of us not notice what the other side is doing, we don't notice what we ourselves are doing. We're so obsessed with the issue at hand that we don't notice the impact of our own behaviour on others. We react to each other but without conscious awareness. The ability to notice how both sides are faring will be addressed in more depth when we look at the third step, Take the Neutral Side.

Principles of behaviour

Taking our own side involves talking about our needs, wants, feelings and thoughts about the topic at hand. It also involves talking about the *way* the topic is discussed: what level of conflict we will tolerate and what works for us. Knowing how you want to communicate is as important as knowing what you want to say. What are your ground rules for conflict? I like to call them principles, rather than rules. Here are some that may be useful to you:

- share the airtime equally
- don't cut people off when they're talking
- no sarcasm or put-downs
- don't dominate the conversation
- keep to the point
- respect different viewpoints

Having discussed the importance of expressing our feelings, we also need to decide what's appropriate to reveal. If we're in an encounter with a business associate, it's probably not appropriate to share our deepest feelings. Business experts usually advise putting feelings aside and using the rational mind. They suggest getting clear about your interests and bottom-line and keeping your emotions out of it.

This is all very well for impersonal contacts and formal encounters, but for intimate relationships it is too impersonal. Some issues may be worked out this way, but many will not. In intimate relationships, revelation of your feelings is key. I also think the workplace can be an appropriate place to air feelings and that the failure to do so blocks a lot of individuals and teams from reaching their potential. Many issues impact upon us emotionally, whether we want them to or not. Sharing what we feel, as opposed to sharing only intellectual ideas, creates connection between people. Connection between people creates possibilities for change, and change opens the door to innovation.

Story: Taking care of business

Finding our voice as employers is an increasingly important issue for women as we branch out into the world of business. This story shows a woman struggling to take her own side in a conflict with an employee.

Jodie was a forty-year-old single woman who planned to open a clothing boutique and was doing extensive renovations for the new store. Her male contractor was hard to communicate with, so Jodie hired a male business consultant to help her take care of negotiations with the contractor and other workmen. But she found that she couldn't deal with the male consultant either! Not only could she not understand the technical language of the contractor, she wasn't getting the emotional support she needed from the consultant.

Jodie was a brave woman going into business on her own but experienced herself as a victim. She felt resentful of other women whose husbands helped and protected them. Jodie felt disadvantaged without a male partner to help equalise the playing field. She needed support but she didn't know where to find it.

Jodie came to my conflict resolution class for help. She looked tough, with short, cropped hair and a loud, outspoken manner, but in fact she was extremely sensitive to criticism. She felt frustrated by her inability to assert herself.

Jodie said she used to be 'angry and tough' when she was young. As she said this, she slammed one fist into the other, showing the angry nature of her former self. *Bam!* 'I was like that!' she said with gusto. I could still see a lot of that anger in Jodie now, but she assured me she had mellowed immensely and that she now detested her former angry self. 'I used to fight, but now I flee.' She attributed this change to years spent in therapy getting in touch with her tender feelings and vulnerability. She was proud of her growth.

Jodie had made a decision that it was better to be soft and open rather than angry in life. This may have been wise, but the fact remained she *was* angry right now. Furthermore, her anger was a potential source of power for her in this situation, but she had decided not to use it. To Jodie it felt too dangerous and overwhelming, like slipping back into an earlier, less mature self.

Along with the problems with her male employees, Jodie was irritated with her newly hired assistant, Meg. Jodie said she felt unsupported by Meg in the store and that Meg reminded Jodie of her former angry self, which bothered her because she no longer agreed with being angry in life. She tried to ignore

Meg's youthful brashness. After all, Jodie had been an angry young person herself at one time. It was interesting that Jodie had hired a young woman who possessed the very energy she now denied but needed in herself. It was time for Jodie to find a way to use this vital energy again, but now as a mature woman.

I created a role-play with Jodie to work on the problem. I suggested she first deal with the issue with Meg because it was least threatening and because developing a support system was Jodie's most vital need at this time. Meg had been employed expressly for this purpose, after all. I asked Jodie to practice taking her own side with Meg. Jodie complained to me that the young and abrasive Meg made her feel inadequate, just as the men did. I suggested she tell Meg how she felt. After much hesitation and grumbling, Jodie said, 'There's tension between us and we have to talk.' I congratulated her on taking this first step into conscious conflict.

When Jodie finally approached Meg in reality and said the things she needed to say, Meg was surprised but also relieved that Jodie was confiding in her. Meg took the opportunity to confide to Jodie in return that she was having difficulties in her personal life and was concerned she might be taking her frustrations out on the job. Jodie's courage created an opportunity for Meg to talk about her difficulties. They began a more co-operative relationship, with Meg now clear on what Jodie wanted from her – support. Jodie had exercised her authority as an employer, a new growing edge for her. She got what she wanted from Meg without losing it.

Jodie's task was to find her voice as the authority of her own business. She began by taking her own side with her new employee. Jodie found out she was not the raging monster she feared, but a balanced and assertive person.

The next step was to deal with the contractor. Sometimes people need to form coalitions or support systems, as Jodie did with Meg, when a party is perceived as too powerful to take on single-handedly. From developing a supportive relationship with Meg, and from learning the skills of taking her own side, Jodie was able to effectively communicate her needs to the contractor. She quit using the consultant. I recommend using conflict resolution where it feels least threatening first and working outwards from there to more threatening conflicts.

Jodie's story shows us how difficult it can be to take your own side. She needed to move through the layers of fear and disbelief until she got to the essence – the emotional centre – of her side. When we find our side, we often feel relieved and think: 'That's it! That's what I wanted to say. I finally said it.'

The wrong way to get what you want

Melissa was a woman who always took her own side. But she never took it effectively. Worse still, she never took the other side. Whenever she didn't get what she wanted she became emotional and blaming. She would persist in her viewpoint until she wore down the other side. Often she got what she wanted, at least on the superficial level, but she lost the love and respect she deeply craved. She had no idea how to resolve a conflict, only how to start one. Melissa's behaviour is an example of the attention-seeking that happens when we are cut off from our true source of power.

We all know people like Melissa, women who use their emotionality and anger to force others into giving them what they want. This is not taking your side. This is being destructive and coercive. A woman like this needs to learn that she can get her needs met without blaming or attacking others, without playing the role of victim or casting every conflict partner as her abuser. She needs to learn that it's only when she communicates her needs in fair and constructive ways that others will feel motivated to meet them.

We can all have a little Melissa in us at times and try to manipulate others into giving us what we want. But resolving our differences with others means having the emotional maturity to accept 'no' for an answer.

Develop the ability to compromise

Melissa didn't have the capacity to take no for an answer, nor was she able to create compromise. A compromise is when each side gets some of what they want but not everything. Sometimes this is the best outcome that can be achieved. It is a process of give and take. A compromise works best when there is a sense of equity in the exchange and when it is clear what people are both giving and receiving. Compromise can be a great learning opportunity, for it reveals what is truly important to each side and what they can afford to let go.

Healing ourselves by taking our own side

There is great power in women coming together to learn about conflict resolution, what it takes and what it costs, and how to create more rewarding relationships with partners, friends, relatives and work associates. Things *are* changing. Women have travelled a long hard road to have their voices heard and honoured.

The ripple effect

When you take your own side in a conflict, all your relationships improve. I have discovered an interesting fact: when we deal well with one person, it has positive effects on our other relationships. Many of the moods we carry around with us have to do with problems we are trying to avoid.

Story 1: The bossy teacher

Joan, a client of mine, complained for weeks about a teacher at her college who had a rude and dismissive attitude. It upset and angered Joan, and this affected the mood between Joan and her boyfriend. The assignment I gave Joan was to talk to her teacher. She did it and it had wonderful effects. It took work to get her teacher to listen, as they debated their viewpoints back and forth, but the teacher did get the point. The teacher even made a public apology to her class for her abrupt manner and began relating to her class with more sensitivity. Many people in the class were very happy with the change, as they too had been suffering and had been gossiping about her. One of the students came up to Joan after class and said, 'Wow, she really changed. Did someone speak to her?' That was a resolution from which everyone benefited: not just Joan, but the other students, the teacher, and Joan's boyfriend, who was happy when Joan's mood improved. That's the ripple effect in action.

Story 2: The writing class

Here is another example of the ripple effect. I was in a small weekly creative writing group for six months. At first I enjoyed it but as time went by, I became more and more anxious. I felt pressured to write great pieces every week and found myself becoming blocked in my writing. I began complaining to a friend that I didn't want to go anymore, but felt I had to out of some unspoken commitment to the group. I worried I would be letting everyone down if I left. Nonetheless, I couldn't put away my feelings of unease and dissatisfaction. I didn't want to say so, but I felt I was finished with the group and needed to move on. It had given me something wonderful but had outworn its usefulness.

My friend suggested that I deal with my inner conflict and not just continue with the group out of a sense of duty. That night I called the three other people in the group and shared my feelings. I took my own side. To my surprise, the response was very positive. In fact, two of the other people felt the same as me! What I had been feeling was not just my own problem, but also something real going on in the group. I had a great conversation with everyone and as a result the group decided to disband but to stay in touch as we felt the need. One of the people said I had been courageous to bring up the issue and take a stand. I had taken a stand and it benefited others. And I was in a better mood at home too! That is the ripple effect.

Get support and create allies

If you have trouble taking your own side or are faced with an intimidating person, get support to take your side. Allies are people who believe in you and your ability to take positive action in your life. They can be friends, relatives, co-workers, therapists, coaches or partners. Ask your ally to help you take your side in an upcoming conflict. They can help you by discussing the issues with you until you get clear about your side. They can do role-plays with you, so you can practise dealing with the challenging person. They can also help you get clear about your goals. Your ally is also there for you afterwards to support your learning and growth. Knowing you have support on your side can give you the power you need to deal with conflict.

If the situation still feels too intimidating, don't do it alone. Get a mediator to help facilitate the discussion.

Implications of women taking their own side

Taking your own side is not only a personal achievement. When you take your own side in a conflict, you are representing a position that has a wider significance, no matter how apparently trivial the incident. Behind most conflicts are issues of power, control, justice and fairness. For instance, when you fight about who takes out the garbage you are actually having a conflict about fairness and equality in the relationship or household. The garbage is a symbol for a deeper issue with social significance – who does the housework. With almost every couple I have ever worked with, this is a major issue and often a fatal one. Who takes responsibility for the housework? Whose needs come first? Who is more successful in getting their needs met?

I recall a young woman crying in my office because she could not get her husband to help with household chores despite the fact that they both held fulltime jobs. As a result she rarely wanted sex with him and doubted whether or not she loved him anymore. That is how critical these issues can become. In Chapter 11, Domestic Hotspots: Housework, Money and Sex, I explore these domestic conflicts in more detail.

Remember, conflict is a concentrated field of energy – tension – wrapped around a specific issue, such as garbage disposal or housework. As we unwrap that bundle of tension, all sorts of other related issues emerge – feeling overworked and taken for granted, tiredness, money problems, divisions of labour and fairness.

Stepping into tension is a courageous act. You may never climb Mount Everest or fly solo across the Atlantic but you can bravely tackle tension in your relationships. Transforming the world begins from where we are in the moment – dealing with the tensions in our own lives.

Exercise: Taking your own side

The goal of this exercise is to take your own side. It requires making every effort to 'win', without concern for the other side. Once you have gone all the way on your side, you are free to change sides and consider the other position. But for now, try being a passionate advocate for your side only. Go ahead and win. You might want to record your responses to the following questions for future reference.

1. Think of a conflict or tension you have with someone in which you find it's hard to take your own side, speak up or be heard.
2. Notice how you feel when you think of speaking up or taking your side. How does it feel not to be able to speak freely?
3. What holds you back? Is there a fear or limiting belief present?
4. What new positive belief could help you in this moment?

Make it bold and dramatic. Say this new belief out loud.

5. Now imagine expressing your side fully – your needs, feelings, ideas. Express your side by saying it out loud or writing it down. Take your time. You have all the time you need.

6. What's it like to finally express your side? What kind of woman are you being when you express your side?

7. What have you learned about yourself through this exercise?

Thoughts to hold

- It's important to take your own side to find resolution.
- Taking your own side is a courageous and powerful act.
- You take your own side by speaking about your needs and wants, thoughts and feelings.
- Women often discover their side through talking it over with others.
- Getting in touch with your feelings can help you discover your side.
- It can take time to know your side. Buy time if you need to.
- Discover what limiting beliefs holds you back from taking your side. Create new, bold and powerful beliefs.

4 Take the Other Side: Listening

The fabric of the new society will be made of nothing more or less than the threads woven in today's interactions.

Pam McAllister, *Reweaving the Web of Life*

In Chapter 3 we learned the importance of Taking Our Own Side. We looked at some of the fears and beliefs that make this difficult for women, and we identified strategies for taking our own side more effectively. It is now time to consider *Taking the Other Side*.

Connection through listening

Taking the other side is more than just simple listening. It is the ability to feel empathy and show respect. When we focus our deep attention on someone and listen with our hearts as well as our heads, we are giving a powerful gift. Listening is a powerful act. It transforms the moment. It connects us as humans. It allows solutions to emerge. It takes the conversation deeper. It builds trust. We do all this when we listen and are fully present. We make resolution possible when we understand the other side. This is how we build relationship – by connecting with the other person. This is the beauty and benefit of taking the other side. It is a reaching out, an extension of ourselves to another. That is strength. That is power.

Women's gift in conflict: big, beautiful, sensitive ears

Traditionally women have been assigned the task of taking care of the 'feeling atmosphere' of relationships and families. This sensitivity to others, empathy and understanding are all important elements in taking the other side. Often women have an uncanny capacity to understand the feelings of others and to see things from someone else's point of view. 'Women's intuition' may be largely related to this capacity to see and hear others.

- In many ways this skill makes women natural facilitators. Women understand that conflict can destroy relationships, families and communities. The skills of empathising, listening and supporting have been largely undervalued in the male-dominated business world. But today, these skills are being incorporated into businesses, as corporations hire trainers for in-house courses on active listening, teamwork, collaboration, coaching and customer service. These are skills that require sensitivity and respect for other people's thoughts, needs and opinions, as well as one's own. The corporate world is discovering that traditional 'feminine' communication skills can improve business.

Taking the other side helps us become wise

There are many benefits of taking the other side such as building trust and understanding and forging connection with others. Often we find it hard to listen to the other side because our egos don't want to open up to another point of view. We don't want our reality to be challenged. We don't want to change. Taking the other side requires a willingness to change – to be influenced by another perspective.

Taking the Other Side is what makes conflict resolution different from assertiveness training. It demands more of us than just speaking up. It requires listening, and learning, and being willing to change. In the process we develop our communication skills and become more open and flexible. We become collaborators in change. We also develop a vision in which difference is honoured and relationship is valued more than winning.

It is only when *both* sides have expressed themselves that resolution can occur. Once each side has revealed itself, real conversation can happen, as we move beyond surface defensiveness. Many times I have thought that what my conflict partner was saying was wrong. I would sit there thinking, 'Do I have to listen to this? Give me a break!' But if I listened carefully and let them express their side, I would get curious. I wanted to know more, understand more. By following my curiosity, I often had an eye-opening experience. I suddenly saw their point of view! Then I would think, 'Wow. I'm glad I hung in there. I nearly missed out on this!' Their reality suddenly seemed to make sense. I nearly missed out on a powerful lesson. Now I knew them more deeply. I may even have increased my wisdom about human nature. Wise people, I have noticed, are always people who listen well.

Story: The case of the ex-husband

Carol was the mother of a seven-year-old boy, Nick. She had married young to Fred, a negative, critical man. She finally divorced him and received sole custody of Nick. Fred had visitation rights.

Carol came to me for help because Fred was driving her crazy. He was angry about the loss of custody of his son and wanted to spend more time with Nick and have more say in raising him. He appealed the initial custody ruling and the court-appointed psychologist recommended that Fred's visitation rights be extended.

Carol resisted Fred's desire to spend more time with Nick, though Fred phoned her repeatedly and criticised her mothering. Carol spent hours on the phone arguing with him and justifying her way of raising Nick. It seemed Carol was unable to take her own side effectively with Fred, getting drawn into endless, fruitless arguments on the phone. I suggested that she refuse to participate in these arguments and instead be firm about not letting him put down her way of raising Nick. It is healthy self-care to stop negotiating when someone continues to be negative or abusive.

Taking her own side more strongly helped to some extent but Fred continued to criticise the way Carol was raising Nick. She wanted Fred out of her life but the truth was she couldn't get rid of him.

We reviewed the situation once more and agreed that while taking her own side worked somewhat, it was not the solution.

I suggested she take *his* side and that she be supportive of him, rather than resisting him. This meant that Carol needed to own the power she possessed. Carol felt like a victim in the situation, not a powerful woman. In truth, she was a powerful woman. She had custody of Nick, was independently wealthy, and was in a new relationship with a new man. She had become pregnant again, which she was thrilled about.

Instead of fighting unproductively, I suggested she take Fred's side for a change. How about truly supporting Fred's need for contact with Nick? How about allowing him to have a positive relationship with his son? At this point, Carol admitted she wanted Nick to hate his father, even though Nick enjoyed time with his father and Fred was a loving father to Nick. The idea of Nick and his father being close brought up deep fears that she would become less close to Nick. She admitted that being a mother meant she didn't have to think about herself. She could look after others and never have to deal with her own development as an individual. The truth was, though bright and creative, Carol was afraid to do develop her skills and talents. Fred's pushing to have more contact with Nick aroused this conflict within herself about who she was. What would she do with herself if Nick spent more time with his father? If she wasn't a mother, who was she?

Carol kept the war going by denying Fred's point of view. In her mind, he was all bad. But by taking Fred's side, Carol discovered that what she most feared was losing her central role as a mother. It was an irrational fear, as she would still be a mother not only to Nick but also to her soon-to-be newborn.

Refusing to take someone's side enrages that person who longs to be heard, no matter how odious they seem to us. As this was going to be a lifetime connection of co-parenting, finding some level of co-operation was highly desirable. Carol's decision to listen to Fred's needs was not giving in, but a conscious choice based on reviewing the matter at length. Carol said she had never taken Fred's side before, in all their post-marital battles. She was so sure she was the victim but in fact she had the power in this situation.

She decided to take his side and to work on her fear of spending more time without Nick. She knew that it wasn't healthy for Nick to be caught in this tug-of-war. By working on her own fears, she could see Fred in a more human light and work towards ending the war between them. This decision to see his side came when she let go of her sense of victim-hood and felt her own strength. It also came out of wanting to take responsibility for her role in the ongoing hostilities.

As Carol supported Fred's need to be a father to Nick, their communication became less combative and more productive. Carol displayed great maturity by looking squarely at her role in keeping the war going. Taking Fred's side was an opportunity for Carol to step into her power and discover a new way of handling her relationship with her ex-husband. She no longer viewed herself as a helpless young woman putting up with a critical ex-husband. She now saw herself as a powerful woman capable of supporting her son's relationship with his father.

When we feel strong in ourselves we feel strong enough to take the other side.

Taking the other side honours the principle of fairness

Fairness means that each side receives equal consideration. Everyone deserves to be treated fairly. During conflict, when tempers are flaring, we often think only of ourselves. We know we should fight fair but often can't resist venting our spleen. We refuse to listen and want to have our way. We don't want to take the other side.

When we violate the rules of fairness, the conflict resolution process breaks down. One reason we stop being fair is that we get hurt or offended or threatened and lose our centre. We stop acting fairly and responsibly.

When we can no longer be fair or take the other side, we need to stop the conflict and address the reason why. We are probably feeling hurt. If this is so, share your hurt feelings honestly with your conflict partner. If that is not possible, return to the conflict at a later time when you are feeling centred and whole again.

Whenever you feel you are not being fair, stop and take the other side. They will appreciate your attempts to be fair.

Taking the other side expresses our gratitude for the existence of others

What a lonely world it would be if other people didn't exist. We need other people. We need their thoughts, feelings, opinions, ideas and knowledge. We need their love and support. We can achieve very little in life without the help of others. We have much to be grateful for. Taking the other side is recognition of the fact that we need others to solve our problems. We need their help and are grateful to them for contributing to our lives. Everyone has information for us. Every time we take the other side we are acknowledging how much we value other people.

Taking the other side produces results

Often our conflict partner raises issues that we overlook. Without the insight they bring to the table, we might make a poor decision or a less effective one. Our conflict partner helps us to be aware of the many options for resolution. The best decisions are those that reflect the ideas of both sides.

Why we don't want to understand the other side

With all the benefits of taking the other side, why do we have difficulty with it? Surprisingly, women often do not use their strong skills effectively in conflicts. When I started teaching my women's conflict resolution classes, I had anticipated women having difficulty taking their *own* side, but I was completely taken aback when they protested bitterly about having to take the *other* side! I found it surprising that, despite our training in caring for others, women often had a great resistance to this step. Upon reflection, however, I realised there were important reasons for this. One of the most common reasons women find it hard to take the other side (and we do find it hard, despite our empathic natures) is that we feel we have given too much already. When we live our lives as chronic givers, we often end up feeling depressed, tired or angry. A lifetime of self-denial doesn't lead to selflessness, but to resentment. It's easier to take the other side when we feel confident our side will be heard and that our needs will be met in conflict.

Here is a list of the most common reasons why we are unable to take the other side.

1. **You haven't taken your own side enough:** You're unable to support the other side because you still haven't got your point across. If this is your situation, return to step one: take your own side. Try to say what you mean until you feel satisfied you've been heard. When you feel heard, you will feel freer to focus on the other side. Often we need to express what we are feeling in order to have space to listen.

   Who should express themselves first? Who should listen first? Usually, the person who has the complaint expresses their side first. If no one person is initiating the complaint, then whoever is most ready or most emotionally charged goes first.

2. **The other side hasn't taken their own side enough:** Whenever you find yourself unable to take the other side, ask yourself why. If you can't take their side, it might be because they haven't said enough to convince you or move you. If this is the case, encourage them to take their side again. After all, you can't take the other side if there's nothing to take. Help them complete their message by encouraging them to go further. Ask for more information until you understand the essence of their message. Here is a list of questions you can ask to help your conflict partner clarify their side:
   - What do you want?
   - How do you see this happening?
   - How do you feel about that?
   - What else is on your mind?
   - Can you tell me more about that?
   - How do you see us reaching an agreement?

- What are other possibilities?
- What is important to you about that?
- What would make you happy?

3. **You are standing for a non-negotiable principle:** Another reason you might have trouble taking the other side is because the issue is non-negotiable for you. You feel this is the one place where you cannot be flexible. You can't compromise because you are fighting for a deep cause, perhaps an ethical principle or a personal choice on which you cannot move. Then be very clear that this is a non-negotiable issue and accept the consequences. I once worked with a couple who were not yet married but were already conflicting about whether or not to have children. He didn't want children. She did. She realised this was a non-negotiable issue for her. He realised he wasn't going to change his mind in the foreseeable future. She realised she was unwilling to wait in hopes of him changing. They parted ways. Some issues are non-negotiable and must be stood for.

- What issues are non-negotiable for you?
- Are you willing to stand for them and accept the consequences?

4. **Old baggage and evening the score:** You feel it's time to change the balance of power in your favour. You are tired of being such a pushover and want to show them you're not taking it any more.

   Nicole lives on the coast communing with birds, trees and the sounds of waves crashing. Normally gentle and generous, she says she resists taking the other side when she fights with her partner, Damian. She refuses to admit her wrongdoings or limitations and will not concede a thing because she feels that as a woman she has been made to admit fault too many times. She gets stubborn and locked into her principle, 'I will not yield anymore!'

Nicole may be more extreme than most, but we all feel like this at times. Nicole says that when she is in those moods it takes her at least two days before she can relent and begin to see the other side. It takes time to see the other side when we are stubborn.

Sometimes we cannot be flexible. We have seen everyone's side but our own for too long. We go on an empathy strike. Often what pours out of women during this stage are stories about *never* being heard, *never* being understood, *never* winning, *never* being allowed to be right. There is a backlog of resentment, anger and pain about always having to take the other's point of view. Refusing to take the other side can feel like a matter of justice. Sometimes it is. Mostly it's about having been the loser in too many previous conflicts.

If you don't at some point find a way to take the other side, the other side will get angry and hopeless. Instinctively, we know that our conflict partner must be heard and that *hopelessness* is the worst thing that can happen in this situation. Hopelessness does not allow for resolution. Hopelessness is a killer of relationship. Don't let your need to even the score destroy the possibility of resolution.

5. **You can't admit to your shortcomings:** Often conflict begins when one person accuses another of some wrong-

doing. We all get accused at times by people who dislike our behaviour or actions. If I could wave my magic wand and give you one skill, it would be the skill of dealing with accusations effectively. If you can master this skill, you can avoid a lot of conflict in your life.

When someone accuses us of something, it is important to take time to consider what aspect of it may be true, without getting lost in guilt or denial. Some accusations are simply hurtful criticisms and should be rejected, but others may have a kernel of truth to them.

Learning to consider others' accusations without defensiveness is one of the most important skills of conflict resolution. As we get more confident at taking our own side, admitting to our shortcomings is less upsetting. It's like looking into a mirror and seeing things we never saw before. 'Do I really do that?' we ask. We all have something to gain from examining the accusations people make about us. We gain awareness of our impact on others.

Jenny had been accused by two co-workers of being 'cold'. Her close friends knew her as warm and sensitive. This negative feedback from her co-workers bothered her greatly, as it conflicted with her image of herself. I immediately saw that Jenny wasn't cold in the slightest. She was shy. But I could also see that this shyness led Jenny to behave in a self-protective and somewhat withdrawn manner around people she didn't know well, including me at first. I could see how people might find her reserved or cool. Jenny was horrified that people found her cold.

While working on this issue, Jenny recalled an incident from childhood in which she and another girl got into a big fight in the schoolyard. Her friend called her ugly names but Jenny couldn't respond; she had been raised to be polite. She felt like an animal frozen with fear, unable to defend itself against a large predator.

Through exploring this story, it became clear that the injunction to 'be polite' had interfered with Jenny's ability to take her own side in life. She was unassertive. Her inner strength took the form of 'coldness' or 'reserve' which was Jenny's unconscious way of protecting herself in the world. She needed to consciously own the part of her that was self-protective and not so polite. As she developed this part of herself, she became less shy and more assertive. Ironically, this allowed her to be warmer and more open with others, knowing she was free to defend herself if necessary. Her entire range of self-expression opened up. I admired Jenny because she had the curiosity and self-love to learn from people's feedback.

When someone accuses you of something, ask yourself:

- How is this true about me?
- How could I become more conscious of this part of me?

6. **You have inner issues that need healing:** When you cannot take the other side or see the other person or issue clearly it is sometimes because inner issues are preventing you. There may be past abuse issues that affect your perception or your ability to participate in constructive conversation. Abuse injures our instincts and intuition and makes it harder to see ourselves and others clearly. While we all have a tendency to blame others and refuse to change, for some people it's a serious block in relationship. If you find you are constantly

unable to see the other's point of view and are often angry with them, you may need individual counselling to help you understand the source of your anger and what is blocking you from understanding the other side.

7. **You like being right:** Often we want to be right in order to feel good about ourselves and in control of the situation. We want the other person to be wrong and to change.

    When we need to be right, we cannot listen to the other side or see another perspective. We tend to judge others harshly for their mistakes. Needing to be right is a major impediment to resolution. Hanging on to being right does not resolve conflict.

    One way to get over this need to be right is to think that both sides are right – both sides have a piece of the puzzle but viewed from different angles. Another way is to tell yourself that being wise is better than being right. A wise person never insists on being right. A wise person prefers to listen and learn and is willing to adjust their viewpoint, depending on the information they receive.

8. **You get hurt and shut down:** Another thing that prevents us from being able to hear the other side is getting hurt. We all get hurt at times. Incidents that touch on deep wounds can send us into hiding where we lick our wounds for many hours. This is a painful place to be. It is doubly difficult when both parties feel hurt at the same time. The atmosphere can become thick with pain and resentment. What can be done? Naming what is happening is the first step and can act to dispel some of the negative atmosphere. Say:

'We're both feeling hurt and angry. Let's take a break for a while,' or, 'I'm hurt and can't hear you right now'.

Sometimes we just can't hear the other side because we are tired and need a break. It is all right to stop and cool off: think, write, take a walk, have a cup of tea, talk to yourself in the mirror, consult a friend, read an inspirational book, throw the runes or call your therapist or coach. Bring yourself back to your centre in the ways that work best for you. Often it is necessary to stop in the midst of conflict to rest and recover. When you have regained your energy and perspective, come back and finish up what you started.

9. **Plain old denial:** Sometimes we can't take the other side because we are in denial and unable to see how our behaviour affects others.

Story: Sylvia and Vivienne

Sylvia and Vivienne were good friends who went to a beach cottage for the weekend. Sylvia woke up after a refreshing nap to hear Vivienne storm into the room snapping loudly about how she 'has to do all the cleaning around here!'. Sylvia's peaceful rest ended abruptly. She felt confused about Vivienne's reprimand. It reminded her of her father, who would walk into a room and bark about something she had done wrong, a common occurrence in her family of origin. Sylvia immediately jumped up and began cleaning up the kitchen and didn't stop until the job was done. She responded as if she were a bad child, not a grown woman who had just been treated disrespectfully by her friend.

Sylvia wanted to work on this incident between them, as she

now felt wary of Vivienne, and also disturbed by her own frightened response. She took her own side first by re-telling her side of the story. Vivienne did not recall the incident at first, and when she did, she said she had only been joking – she hadn't meant it as a reprimand. This denial threw Sylvia off centre – she looked spaced out and seemed unable to assert her side in the face of Vivienne's denial. As I was there to help them work on the conflict, I suggested to Vivienne that she notice the impact of her denial on Sylvia. Vivienne looked at Sylvia's distraught face closely for the first time.

I suggested that Vivienne try taking Sylvia's side. I said, 'Assume she has a good point but it's hard for her to explain it and for you to hear it. Ask her questions. Get her to tell you more about her experience.' I told Sylvia to believe in her perceptions and focus specifically on what bothered her about Vivienne's reprimand that day. 'It was so sudden,' Sylvia said. 'I was just coming out of a deep sleep and my defences were down. She sounded so angry.' Vivienne listened carefully. She admitted, 'I *was* sarcastic in my tone.' Sarcasm is about anger and criticism not expressed directly. Vivienne saw the impact her anger had on Sylvia and the hurt that had been created. She apologised for her behaviour.

I asked Vivienne to explore her anger. She discovered that she felt resentful of Sylvia's freedom and wealth. This admission paved the way for them to talk about other issues in their relationship and led to a deeper honesty for both women.

How to take the other side: Listening

Taking the other side is often experienced energetically as Moving Back. You need to step back to make space for the other person to express their side and for you to receive their information. It is like applying the brakes. You slow yourself down and pull back to make room for the other.

Here are some ways in which we can use our power to make space for the other person, drawing them out and affirming their side. Learn to listen by:

- asking open-ended questions
- being willing to learn about the other side
- honouring difference
- remembering accurately what the other has said
- expressing empathy – feeling into the other person's situation
- admitting when you agree with the other person's point
- encouraging the other side to express themselves
- seeing where their complaints about you are true
- recognising the other person as a mirror of your own strengths and weaknesses

Ask questions and be curious

If you don't feel a connection with your conflict partner, say so and ask for more information until you *can* connect. Never be shy to ask for more information. Inquire and learn about the other side until you click with what they are saying. Sometimes people recoil from being asked questions and can feel invaded, therefore the attitude of the questioner is important. Usually an attitude of respect and sincere curiosity to learn more about the other person is helpful. If you meet resistance to your questions, talk openly about yourself for a while or return to your questions at a later time. If you sincerely ask for more information, you will receive it.

Listen generously

What do you listen for when you listen to someone? There are many things to listen for. Listening *for*, as opposed to listening *to*, is about listening for what someone doesn't say – the spaces in between the words – as well as what they do say. It is about listening with generous ears and hearing what the person wants, where their pain is, what feelings they experience, and what direction they want to go in.

When you are *not* taking the other side

Don't use fake listening

Pretending to listen to the other side and silently thinking '*they're so wrong*' is not taking the other side. We can't fake it. When we take the other side, we need to be genuine. People sense when we are preoccupied with our own thoughts and not truly listening.

If you find yourself trying to listen to the other side but inwardly obsessed with your own thoughts, take your own side as soon as you get a chance. This will help clear your mind enough to listen to others. Alternately, you can put aside your internal chatter and simply become curious about what the other person is saying. Allowing yourself to be curious can lead to all sorts of unexpected revelations. People will share more deeply of themselves when they sense you are truly listening. They will tell you things you weren't expecting!

Taking the other side is not self-sacrifice

It is important to be clear about the difference between taking the other side, which is a creative and positive act, and sacrificing yourself. Taking the other side is not about conceding and should not feel like submission or pretence. Many women think taking the other side means giving up their own side in order to keep the relationship. They think they have to be stoic and self-sacrificing — a Rock of Gibraltar, silently and patiently nurturing the relationship, while waiting for their partner, friend or relative to understand and appreciate their sacrifice.

When women feel they are sacrificing too much, they are not taking their own side enough. Don't sacrifice your need to be yourself just to keep things smooth at home. This is not resolution. And it helps nothing. Many women never get their creative work done because they are too busy caring for others. If this is your problem, consider your need to take your side more. Your partner and your children need to understand that if you don't get to write the book, paint the painting, make the business deal or have a weekend alone, you will not be able to give them and the world the top-quality love that is yours to give.

Sacrificing your creative and personal development so that others can be supported in their creative pursuits is not resolution, nor a wise investment. It is based on a belief that you have to sacrifice your own needs in order to be loved. This is an inner conflict as well as an outer social conflict for women. Just remember that taking the other side is not sacrifice or surrender. It is the power to connect with others through listening and learning about them.

Story: Using our differences to strengthen us

Christopher and Margaret had a conflict over talking and listening. I noticed early on that Christopher was getting more airtime in the conversation. Margaret sat there in a zombie-like trance pretending to listen to Christopher. This is a very common process for women and men alike – pretending to listen when in fact we are frozen or bored. I have taken an informal poll and many women and men are adept at the art of pretend-listening.

I could see that Margaret was trying lamely to get out of her very 'feminine' role, but none too successfully. She and Christopher got into a heated conflict about talking and listening. Christopher insisted he didn't want to hold himself back just because Margaret couldn't get herself into the conversation. He challenged her to jump into the conversation, to cut him off, interrupt and take the conversation in new directions if she wished. She didn't rise to his challenge. She just sat there, so I asked her why didn't she just jump into the conversation as Christopher suggested. 'How rude that would be!' she said, 'I can't do that! Why doesn't he notice I'm bored or worn out from listening?' She was red in the face when she said this and I could see this issue was truly distressing for her. I asked her to continue taking her side. She railed at Christopher, 'Why can't you be more related to me as the *listener*? Why can't you be more equal in conversation, like my female friends are? Why do I have to fight to get in? Why can't you ask more questions and make space for me?' Christopher countered by saying, 'Margaret, why can't you just speak up and be yourself? Why do I have to hold myself back or make sure I'm perfectly attuned to your needs?' 'But I'm perfectly attuned to yours!' she shot back. 'Well, stop!' shouted Christopher. 'Why don't *you* stop!' yelled Margaret.

To complicate matters, not only did Christopher tend to dominate when it came to talking with Margaret, he also defended his communication style as being a passionate Italian:

highly verbal, forceful and expressive. Margaret felt defeated. Not only did she feel out-matched verbally, but if she complained she was guilty of being culturally insensitive. This is conflict resolution in the twenty-first century: not only are there gender issues that generate conflict, but cultural, class and religious issues have increased as people have close relationships across ethnic, class and religious boundaries.

Who should change? Should Christopher change and become more like Margaret in his style – patient and polite? Or should Margaret become more like Christopher – masculine or 'Italian' in hers? How could they co-exist with their different styles? Ironing out the issues in their communication had become a real challenge.

They were both right about each other's limitations – Christopher's too dominating style, and Margaret's too passive style. They both needed to grow and expand their own communication repertoire. Margaret needed to break out of her role as the polite listener and start taking her own side more, saying when she didn't want to listen, interrupting, redirecting the conversation and generally taking up more space. She worked on this and did change in significant ways. She told me some time later that becoming a 'loud-mouth', as she put it, was more fun than she had imagined. Christopher agreed to improve his listening skills and to notice the impact of his dominating style on Margaret. He also took her side by becoming more aware of the gift of her listening. A new equality entered their communication.

Though it can be difficult, expanding and changing the way we communicate can be gratifying. Often what is needed in chronic conflicts such as Christopher and Margaret's is for both people to take the other side and make the changes the other is requesting of them. When we make this effort, we become stronger and more flexible people.

Wider implications of taking the other side

When we take the other side, we are actually getting in contact with another part of ourselves. For example, Margaret needed to get in touch with her forceful and dominating side. Christopher needed to open up to the side of him that was receptive, relaxed and patient. He also needed to value the role of listener, as he developed this capacity in himself. This is the psychological and spiritual work of conflict resolution – by taking the other side, we open up to aspects of our own humanity appearing in the guise of our conflict partner. When we connect with each other through our differences, whether strengths or weaknesses, we create connection and intimacy. Taking the other side enlarges and strengthens us.

Exercise: Taking the other side

1. Think of a conflict where you find it hard to hear the other side.
2. Imagine taking your own side first as fully as you can. Express everything you want to say. Notice when you feel complete – there will be a sense of relief.
3. Now imagine listening to the other side. What do you hear? What are you curious about? What questions do you want to ask them? What are you learning about them? About yourself?

4. Be on their side fully for a moment and repeat their position clearly and fully, as if you were an advocate for their side. This will also help clarify your own position.
5. What is the most difficult aspect of taking their side?
6. Now, imagine that the other side is an aspect of yourself. What part of you does your conflict partner represent?

Thoughts to hold

- We take the other side by listening to and learning about the other person.
- Asking open-ended questions allows us to get to know someone.
- Repeating back what we hear makes people feel heard.
- Accusations can offer us valuable information about the impact we make on others.
- When we are confident in ourselves it is easier to take the other side.
- When we can't take the other side, it is usually because we haven't taken our own sufficiently.
- Chronic conflict is caused by one or both parties refusing to take the other side.

5 Take the Neutral Side: Seeing

Establishing lasting peace is the work of education;
all politics can do is keep us out of war.

Maria Montessori

Neutrality is the ability to see and get an overview. It is about going to the mountaintop and looking down on the scene below. It's taking the bird's-eye view to gain a new perspective, one that is more impartial and appreciative of both sides.

To take a neutral position during conflict requires being *in* the conflict and *out* of it at the same time. Some people are naturally gifted at being neutral and seeing the overall picture, even while in the midst of the hottest of frays. They can keep one eye on the process and notice when things get off track. But even if this doesn't come naturally, it is something we can all learn to do.

Neutrality allows us to stand back and survey ourselves and the other side as if looking in from the outside. When we are immersed in a conflict we often miss important information because we are so embroiled emotionally. Standing back allows us to study the proceedings and gain new insights and information about ourselves and each other. If taking your own

95

side means voicing your needs, and taking the other side means hearing and learning what the other needs, then taking the neutral side means seeing what the conflict needs to resolve itself.

Taking the neutral side gives the relationship itself a chance to come forward and be heard. By stepping into the neutral role we see where things are stuck (not who is to blame) and where communication is blocked. The neutral position doesn't judge either side. It sees that tempers are frayed or nerves are jangled. It sees that people need appreciation and support, or that deeper emotions are in the background, or that the communication is unbalanced with one person doing all the talking and the other too much listening. It sees that someone is gripped by inner conflict and needs time to focus on his or her own healing, or that one person is confident and cool while the other is a nervous wreck, or that everyone needs a break. It sees all this with compassion and concern.

When do we need to take the neutral side?

When should we step out for a review of the process? There are many moments when it is useful to stop and reflect on how things are proceeding. For instance, we may consider taking a neutral view whenever we are overwhelmed by emotions and we feel the need to centre ourselves again. We can take a break and talk about what has happened so far and whether we want to keep going in that direction.

Sometimes when we feel like withdrawing or disconnecting from the other person, it is an indication that a 'Time Out' is in order. Then we should stand back and take a good look at what is happening and try to determine why we are feeling withdrawn, disconnected or bored. Stepping out to get an overview is important whenever we feel stuck, spaced-out, hopeless or tired – any feeling or state that prevents us from being fully present and active in the process.

Taking the neutral side means being a referee

Taking the neutral side may seem an impossible task when you are deeply embroiled in conflict. But it is actually quite natural. Children do this all the time during play with each other. They stop the game for a moment to argue about some rule or to discuss how the game should proceed, then they launch back into play. This happens in sports as well, when the game is stopped by a referee to enforce a rule or break up a fight.

When we take the neutral side in a conflict, we shift levels from *playing* the game to *examining* the game and how it is proceeding. The object of the game of conflict is for the two sides to find the hidden treasure of resolution. The game is played by having both sides share as much information as they can about what they need, want, feel and think. Extra points are gained by suggesting creative solutions that allow both sides to win. As in any other game, one or both sides will need to take the neutral position in the course of the game to act as referee or guide.

Does true neutrality exist?

When we think of the word neutrality we usually think of things like objectivity, fairness, freedom from emotion or detachment. You may wonder how we can be neutral while also taking our own side. It could be argued that true neutrality doesn't exist, and that we always see things from our own biased position.

It may be true that there is no perfect neutrality or objectivity. However, for purposes of conflict resolution, we can learn to take a relatively non-partisan viewpoint that can see both sides. The neutral side can see what each side is *trying* to express, however imperfect their attempts. Even more importantly, it can see the whole picture, the pattern of communication that is happening between people and where it is stuck.

How can we be neutral in the face of injustice or power differences?

Some people have a philosophical problem with the concept of neutrality, for how can one be neutral in the face of injustice, whether it be war crimes, domestic violence or social oppression? Similarly, in our personal relationships, how can we be neutral about any kind of abuse or power differences? It is important to realise that neutrality is not a denial of power problems or injustice. Neutrality simply acknowledges that both sides have a viewpoint, however difficult or disagreeable to hear. Every one has a right to their opinion and everyone has needs they seek to have met. The neutral position believes everyone deserves to be heard and respected.

When we take the neutral position we take responsibility for ensuring that both sides have their say. We help things get back on track when they stray from the topic at hand. We make sure that the conflict is a fair and clean one, and that no dirty fighting tactics occur on either side, no matter how charged the topic. Taking the neutral side is not about denying or condoning injustice, it is about recognising that both sides have needs and feelings and that the greatest chance for an equitable solution lies in hearing out both sides.

How to take the neutral side: The process of seeing

Neutrality is about being fair and impartial – a friend to both sides – versus being right. It is taking the side of the relationship – being concerned with *we*: how are *we* doing, where are *we* stuck, how can *we* resolve this.

Think of the neutral side as the Fair Witness, someone who can see and understand both sides. The Fair Witness is able to see how each side is faring and is able to communicate what she sees in an objective and supportive manner. The Fair Witness helps us avoid getting so caught up in our own side that we forget about finding a positive solution for all. Here are some ways in which we can use our power to stand back and see the whole as the Fair Witness. The Fair Witness:

- sees the whole and has an overview of the process
- is non-judgmental toward both sides
- sees what is best for the relationship as opposed to either side
- offers constructive comments
- responds to the needs of both parties
- supports both sides
- uses detachment, compassion and humour to support the process

- values learning and relationship-building over winning
- is free to step out of the conflict to view the process

Neutrality is experienced energetically as Stepping Out. We need to step outside a conflict and detach for a moment in order to study the overall process. The neutral position takes hold of the steering wheel and focuses on carefully guiding the car. It asks: Where are we headed? Is this where we want to go? Should we change course?

Having an overview: Meta-communication

Let's suppose you are in a hot conflict with your conflict partner. Things are going nowhere. You see things differently, want different things. You want to move to Melbourne, he wants to stay in Sydney. Things seem to be stuck, so you decide to take the neutral side. You step out, metaphorically speaking, and look at how the conflict is proceeding. From this viewpoint, you can see that you are not listening to each other. You both need to relax and really listen to the hopes and dreams of the other.

You might share this insight with your partner. He agrees. You both agree to continue the conflict but this time to really listen to each other. In this case, each side could then discuss what 'Melbourne', or 'Sydney', means to them, while the other side listens, asks questions and provides emotional support.

This discussion of the overview is very important. It is where a lot of deadlocks get unstuck. If you can agree about the overview, about what is happening and why things are stuck, you are halfway home. You are then starting to work together as a team, to co-operate. You are starting to think about resolution and not just about your side. You are communicating *about* your communication. We call this meta-communication (meta means *beyond*). What is the difference?

Meta-communication is communication a level up from the issue level of the conflict. Meta-communication is a discussion about the discussion. This is important because we all get wrapped up in the issues and forget to talk about how the overall communication is going. Seeing and discussing the overview is neutrality. We stand back and ask ourselves, 'What's going on here? How is the conflict proceeding? How are both sides managing? How do we look and sound? Are we stuck? What do we need to do?'

For example, let's imagine a couple, Lee and Paul, are talking about purchasing opera tickets. Lee says, 'I think we should pay for the tickets out of our joint household expenses account'. That is straight communication. But then Lee says, 'I notice it gets tense between us when we discuss how to pay for the tickets'.

In the first statement, Lee is saying what she wants – she thinks they should pay for the tickets out of the joint household expenses account. In the second, Lee is *talking about the nature of the communication* between Paul and herself – that talking about paying for the tickets creates tension. That is meta-communication. It is talking *about* the communication itself.

Communication System
Neutral Side
What's happening here?

Lee's Side   **Paul's Side**
'Let's pay for the tickets out   *'Let's not!'*
of the joint account'

Discussing how the communication is going is especially necessary when there are patterns (either momentary or long-term) that are keeping the process stuck. Unless this is addressed, discussion about the issue won't make much difference. You have to go to a higher level to see where the stuck place is and get things moving again. Standing back and looking at how things are going can even resolve the problem because it can bring new insight and information that was not seen from the limited viewpoint of each side. After we see where the communication is stuck, we can deal with the issue more easily.

For example, Lee and Paul begin to fight over how the tickets should be paid and cannot agree. Paul thinks they should pay for their own tickets separately. How can such a trivial issue get so heated? What is going on? They decide to stand back and take a neutral view of their communication. They see that Lee seems timid and Paul is annoyed. They set the ticket issue aside for the moment and try to see what deeper issue is making Lee timid and Paul annoyed.

Communication System
Neutral Side
seeing the overview

Lee's Side	Paul's Side
(conscious communication)	*(conscious communication)*
'Let's use the joint account!'	*'Let's each pay for our own ticket!'*
(unconscious communication)	*(unconscious communication)*
'I'm afraid to discuss this with you.'	*'I'm irritated by you.'*

Paul sees that Lee is tentative and not coming straight out with what's truly bothering her. Perhaps we suspect, for example, that Lee can't afford to pay for the tickets out of her own account or that she secretly wants Paul to pay for the tickets but isn't willing to say so directly. Lee sees Paul's irritability, which makes her tentative about telling him what she really wants. Like many couples, they have communication patterns that dovetail perfectly. This means that each person's communication pattern tends to reinforce the pattern of the other party. Another way of saying this is that the way we communicate influences that way someone communicates with us. Change occurs when one or both sides decide to communicate differently. They change the pattern. Lee is put off by Paul's gruffness, so doesn't express herself openly and directly at times. Paul feels irritated by Lee's lack of directness. Neither Lee nor Paul are consciously aware of the timidity and gruffness in their respective styles, though they can clearly see it when it is pointed out to them.

Paul is right in a way. Lee is holding something back. She did suggest they pay for the tickets from the joint household expenses account because her personal cash flow this month is tight. She is struggling with her finances.

Lee is right too. Paul gets irritable when he feels something is not above board. He communicates this through his gruff voice tone and facial expression. Paul also has a habit of checking every bill to be sure he hasn't been over-charged, and he tends to have the final word on their money decisions. He has become something of a money authority in Lee's eyes. He is not aware that his need to be in control triggers the very timidity he finds so irritating in Lee.

After both of them see how their communication is affecting the other, they agree to go on. Lee realises she needs to let go of her fear and say what she really wants: 'Paul, I want to discuss our financial arrangements'. If he remains gruff, she then needs to say, 'Paul, your gruffness scares me'. She needs to say exactly what frightens her: his voice tone, facial expression, attitude towards money.

Paul also needs to communicate more directly instead of getting moody when he feels something is not being said. Furthermore, they do need to talk about money. It might be useful for them to talk about how Paul's greater financial assets make Lee feel less powerful in the relationship in terms of financial decision-making.

Lee and Paul are now working on a deeper level of tension in their relationship. The opera tickets were an unexpected doorway into addressing these deeper issues. The issues of power, decision-making, timidity and gruffness probably play out in other areas of their relationship as well. By stepping away from the ticket conflict for a moment and studying the overall communication, they were able to uncover the under-lying issues. This opened up the opportunity for them to learn much more about each other and eventually to resolve an ongoing conflict between them.

Prepare yourself by taking the neutral side in advance

Feeling neutral is great because it is a pleasantly cool state in which we feel centred and calm. These moments may be infrequent, but they do occur. We often experience them while we are on our own – reading a book in bed at night, folding the laundry, going for a walk or just pondering the universe. These neutral moments are the perfect time to take a tension inventory. While we are feeling nice and cool, we can take a neutral look at any tension spots and dreaded topics, for example: 'John and I avoid talking about sex, and we always get tense when we talk about visiting my parents'. It is helpful to make a list of tensions and decide to work through them gently and gradually over time. It is like slowly pulling out all the weeds that are strangling the garden. We can use our calm states to prepare ourselves for future conflict and discover what are the important issues to focus on. Here are some questions we can ask ourselves:

- What do I want?

- What do I feel about the topic?
- How do I want the other side to change?
- What do I want to get out of this conversation?

- Where am I flexible? Where inflexible?
- How important is this to me?
- How can I change?
- What is hardest to say or hear?

Story: Barbara takes a good look at herself

Barbara had loaned money to a friend for a car and had trouble collecting the loan a year later, as agreed upon. The friend, Clarissa, kept putting off paying back the money, always with watertight excuses. Barbara was understanding of her friend's financial problems but underneath felt afraid of falling out with her if she made trouble. She was scared to ask for her money because she had just entered into a business deal with Clarissa and felt dependent on her goodwill to complete the deal. She didn't want to upset things. Yet she needed the money.

I helped Barbara work on this conflict. She clearly needed help taking her own side. She tried practising it many times but always ended by taking back her words when she felt she had gone too far. After she had role-played the conflict and tried in vain to take her own side, I asked her to stand back and take a neutral look at herself in the conflict. She stood back and replayed the conflict in her mind's eye. She studied herself as if looking at a stranger. She stood there with her hands on her hips, contemplating herself from this detached and cool perspective. From the neutral side she could see that: 'I'm back-peddling all the time'. This was true. Barbara would ask for the money and then say something like, 'But it's okay if you don't have it now – I don't want to pressure you'.

Barbara also saw how tense she was with Clarissa. She realised she often felt intimidated by Clarissa, who struck her as domineering and unsympathetic. Barbara saw that her unresolved feelings about Clarissa were making it more difficult for her to take her own side in the car loan conflict. She knew she would have to deal with these feelings eventually if she were to proceed with the business partnership. In fact, she wondered if she should even be in a business arrangement with Clarissa at all!

After using the neutral view to gain these insights, Barbara practised taking her side again. She was more successful the second time around, having taken the time to study herself and where she was blocked. Taking the neutral side in a cool moment gave Barbara more confidence. She now knew that she had two issues to iron out: one about the car loan and one about the ongoing tension between her and Clarissa. By taking the neutral side Barbara saw that she needed to develop more confidence with Clarissa. She also saw that her decision to enter into a business relationship with Clarissa needed serious reviewing.

Taking the neutral view: things you might see
- Someone is not taking his or her own side sufficiently.
- Someone can't listen and is unable to take the other side.
- There is unequal listening and talking.
- There is a lack of clarity about the issue.
- The conversation is too intellectual. One or both sides need to express their gut feelings.
- It is time to talk about details.
- It is time to take a break.
- It is time to make up.
- Dirty fighting tactics are being used.
- Something is not being said.
- Good ideas for resolution are not being noted.
- Apologies are not being acknowledged.

Be positive!
It is possible for both sides to step out and take a look at what's happening. Two sets of eyes are better than one. However, you can take the neutral side even when the other person can't. You may even be able to teach them how to do this.

Get into the habit of studying yourself in conflict. After a conflict session discuss or write down what you did well and where you weren't so happy with yourself. If your conflict partner is interested, you can do a quick run-down of how each of you did or how you did as a team. Remember, it is a learning experience above all else.

When you take the neutral side, you can remind each side

to breath, keep going, love yourselves, take a break, and cherish the good work you both have done so far. Be positive and constructive!

Taking the neutral side: things you might say

- We need to slow down and listen to each other more.
- You need to take your side more.
- I need to listen to you more.
- We are going around in circles. Let's listen more.
- We are blaming each other. Let's support each other.
- We are tired. Let's take a break.
- I am not taking my side fully.
- We need to own up to our contribution to the problem.
- We need to talk about our feelings more.
- What is the background issue here?
- We're not getting to the root of the problem.

When you are *not* taking the neutral side

Neutrality doesn't mean not caring or acting cold. In fact, it often helps us stop being abusive and to take a kinder view. Taking the neutral side means contacting the wise woman in us, stepping back from our intense involvement and taking a good objective look. It means looking at ourselves, our conflict partner and the relationship with a clear eye. It means dropping our projections for a moment and seeing what is really happening. It means being the Fair Witness – the honest eye, the kind elder, the wise guide and helpful mediator. This Fair Witness doesn't criticise or correct, but says faithfully what she sees and what is needed to get things unstuck and flowing again. For instance, the Fair Witness might see that someone needs to speak up more, or listen more. She might observe that someone looks hopeless, angry, or hurt and is not saying so. She looks to see if the communication is getting too intellectual and guides people back to being more direct. She also notices if there is power imbalance – is one person dominating? Is verbal abuse present? Do people feel unsafe to speak their minds? Is it time to get down to the nitty-gritty? Is it time to stop? Is this an issue that can really be solved right now? Would individual therapy or formal mediation be more suitable?

Don't step into the neutral side and blast your conflict partner!

The neutral side is on everybody's side. That is the meaning of neutrality. It should never spoil its unique position by sneaking in bitter comments like, 'It appears you're stuck'. Resist this! Keep this role clean as if it were a sacred place, a no-fire zone. Don't go for short-term gratification over long-term satisfaction. Invest wisely in your relationships. Stay clean. Stay positive.

Coming to a mutually supportive resolution is a hundred times more satisfying and gratifying than taking a cheap shot and keeping the war going. Hurt is what motivates people to take revenge, to keep fighting. Verbally blowing up your partner doesn't get you understanding or resolution. Being honest and positive does.

Implications of the neutral side for society: Fairness and compassion

Can you imagine living in a world where everyone had the capacity to see beyond their own side? What kind of world would it be where we upheld fairness and equality, and where we took responsibility for the well being of each other?

We are in the midst of a shift in our thinking, from competing and winning, to co-operation and sharing. We are moving from a win–lose model, to a win–win model of relationship. The popular philosophy of win–win literally means that if you win, I win. If you lose, I lose. We are in it together. Success depends on our ability to support one another. This new shift in thinking is a shift to a mode of thinking that is very feminine in nature, where relationship and co-operation is highly valued. As this shift continues to take root in society, women will be at the forefront, helping to make this a more just world.

Taking the neutral side is about becoming a mediator, not only for others, but also for our own conflicts. The world needs more mediators – people who are able to support all sides and promote co-operation and resolution. Mediators are able to listen deeply to the stories and needs each side brings to the table. For all of us, taking the neutral side is an opportunity to step into that part of us that is compassionate, wise, loving and big-hearted. Taking the neutral side is the magic key that opens the door to resolution.

Exercise: Practising neutrality

1. Think of a conflict you have or had with someone.
2. Imagine taking your own side.
3. Imagine what the other side would say.
4. Step out and take the neutral position. What do you see? Report on your observations, for example: 'I notice I am

holding back my feelings', or 'I think it might be helpful to try showing how we understand each other', or 'I think it might be helpful if we went into more details', or 'I think we need to express our needs more directly', or 'I think we need to listen more'.

5. Go ahead and try your suggestion. Did it help?
6. Give yourself feedback. How did you do at seeing the overview? Were you able to be neutral? What stopped you from seeing the overview?

Thoughts to hold

- Neutrality means stepping out and seeing the overall communication pattern.
- We can look to children's games and sports for good examples of taking the neutral side.
- Neutrality is not indifferent or critical. Remember to be positive and constructive in your comments.
- Stepping out and getting an overview can lead to deeper insights about the conflict and yourself.
- Discussing the overview together (meta-communication) helps resolve conflict.
- Compassionate neutrality can change the world.

6 Making Up

*SMILE! We're one day closer to World Disarmament
— and a really big party!*

Anonymous

How do we finish a conflict in a positive way? How do we make up afterwards to ensure the peace and well being of the relationship? How do we make up if resolution wasn't reached? What *can* we do to make up?

After men have conflicted they often shake hands, joke, slap each other on the back or buy each other a beer. When they do this, they are enacting a time-honoured male ritual of reparation.

Often, women simply hug, laugh or cry. Maybe we make a cup of tea or share food together. We talk about a neutral topic. It is a relief to end a conflict. Making up is a joyful moment, and often an emotional one.

Couples often make up with each other by hugging, smiling, joking, going out to dinner together, giving flowers, cards, notes, leaving phone messages and by making love.

In a business relationship, people smile, joke, shake hands, exchange formal thanks, acknowledge each other or have their secretary send flowers, notes of thanks, or offer a gift or service.

Think for a moment about how you make up with the various people in your life.

What's so important about making up?

Making up is the magical fourth step and very important for conflict resolution. It puts everything back in its place after the upheaval of conflict. It returns the world to normal and harmonises the relationship again. It is the part of conflict resolution that is completely about taking care of and restoring the relationship. It is about ending on a positive note. Even if the conflict didn't reach a resolution and you still haven't come to any solutions together, you can still make up for now, knowing that things are not complete and will need completing later.

If you feel confident about your skills of making up, it is easier to conflict in the first place. You know how to bring things to a positive close after it is over. My mentor used to say that it is okay to conflict if you know how to clean it up afterwards, but most of us are unsure and insecure about how to clean up the mess of conflict. How do we repair bruised egos? How do we heal the awkwardness between us and the other party? Is it worth going into conflict if it creates more mess in life? The simple answer is 'No'. There is no point getting into a conflict and then walking away from it, leaving another mess on the planet. If we enter a conflict we need to see it through to the end, even if it takes several sessions. We need to take responsibility for the clean up job. Making up is the way to clean up. It seals the resolution, locks it in place.

In order to have a conflict, we need to accept the fact that there will probably be a little momentary mess, a little awkwardness. After all, we are addressing a tension spot and looking for ways to resolve it. What creates resolution is hanging in there and finishing the process, not just slinging a few rounds of mud and then walking off in a huff, hoping someone else will make it better. We need to make sure our conflicts are put to good use as rich fertiliser for our growing relationships.

How to make up: The power of smiling

Making up is about dissolving any last remaining tension that exists. We can't always dissolve all the tension in a conflict but we can considerably reduce it. Making up allows us to reduce it even further before parting ways or moving on to something else. Its purpose is to reduce tension, care for the relationship, and restore the positive self-image of each person.

Making up is experienced energetically as a smile. Sometimes it is literally experienced as a hug. But whether it takes the form of a smile, a bow, a hug, a handshake, or caring words, the energy is felt as warm, friendly and positive. A smile indicates warmth and goodwill. It dissolves tension. It's like pulling the car off the road to have a breather and appreciate a beautiful view. It relaxes and restores.

Here are some ways in which we use our power to make up and restore peace and goodwill. You can honour each other by:
- appreciating the other person
- acknowledging the other person for who they are and what they do
- being grateful for the connection
- giving thanks for the time and effort you both gave

- apologising for any hurts, insults or misunderstandings
- offering to do something to restore goodwill
- using humour to dissolve any remaining tension
- stating the positive gains that came out of the meeting

The two best skills for making up: Apology and image repair

Apology: A gift from the heart

An apology, genuinely felt and expressed, is one of the most powerful things we can do in a conflict. It does a lot to resolve a conflict at the feeling level. Unfortunately, it is quite rare to receive a genuine apology. But apology is a true gift of making up. Even if we don't feel we did anything technically wrong, offering our apologies can restore good feeling. At the end of a conflict, when we are ready to make up, it is helpful to say we are sorry simply because conflict sometimes hurts or feels difficult. Conflict takes time and effort and often puts our noses out of joint. An apology is a way of acknowledging the discomfort of the process and caring for our conflict partner's feelings.

Saying we are sorry in a heartfelt and timely manner acknowledges our part in the problem. Of course, when we feel we had no part in the problem, we cannot apologise for that. However, often we say or do things that are *part* of the problem, even when we don't mean to.

The most important thing about an apology is that it must be clean and heartfelt. There are no 'buts' to an apology. There are no excuses or rationalisations. We need to give the apology freely and fully and let it go.

An apology is a unique and powerful act. It should stand alone, uncomplicated by other messages. It should be a gift of amends that the other side can receive easily and fully. We should give the apology, then be quiet and wait for the other side to speak. The other side can accept it or not. If they do not accept our apology, we can simply say that we apologise anyway and also accept their feelings. They may feel like accepting it later in the privacy of their own hearts.

It is only human to err: It is important to own our mistakes and make amends where possible. Many people cannot humble themselves and remain defensive to the end. This prevents resolution. Acknowledging our mistakes is an excellent skill that prevents us from acting rigid and superior. It shows great humility, flexibility and character. It is an act of graciousness that others appreciate enormously.

One of the great benefits of being able to acknowledge our mistakes is that we can afford to take risks. If we can accept that we will make mistakes, we are freer to learn and try new things. This acceptance of our own fallibility makes it possible to say 'I was wrong', 'I made a mistake', or 'I blew it, I'm sorry', sincerely, but without guilt or shame.

Owning our mistakes and errors also models to others how they should respond to our imperfection. If we openly accept our mistakes, we disarm others who are attacking us with criticism. The more fully you can admit to your mistakes in an open and direct manner, hiding nothing, the less you will be attacked for them. Sometimes you can admit your mistakes in a lighthearted manner. At other times it is important to express regret.

If, after we have apologised fully, our partner continues to attack us, we should object to this. We should never be punished or demeaned for honest mistakes. Unfair character attacks should be stopped immediately. If our intention was not to hurt someone, our apology should be happily accepted. If we did do something to deliberately hurt someone, that is another story, and something for us to look at more deeply.

Here are sample statements for apologising:

- I made a mistake, sorry.
- I'm sorry, I made an error.
- I'm sorry it didn't work out.
- I'd like to make it up to you.
- Yes, you were right all along.
- I'm sorry for any inconvenience.
- I apologise for the pain I caused you.
- I'm sorry this process was difficult for you.
- I apologise for my lack of understanding.

When apology runs amok: Some women apologise for *other* people's errors and mistakes. The classic example is the woman who apologises to someone who steps on her foot. For some women, making mistakes reinforces the cruel conditioning they received that they are stupid or incompetent. They apologise all the time because they feel inferior and insecure and are terrified of offending anyone. In these cases, apology needs to be used sparingly. Apology should be a gift, not a grovel. It should stand up and shine, not crawl. If we find ourselves saying we are sorry or admitting all the blame in every conversation, something is wrong. We need to take our own side more. In this case, we need to practise not saying 'I'm sorry', and see what happens.

Image repair: Restoring each other's positive face

Knowing how to repair any dings and damage to the self-image of our conflict partner is very important. Losing face is a painful experience for most people, and if not addressed it can set the stage for ill will, possibly even covert desires for revenge.

We all lose face when we conflict. Most of us are not at our best during conflict. We look hot under the collar, we stumble, we deny, we clam up, we get rude or say hurtful things, we get stuck, we get angry and emotional, we make mistakes, we don't know what the solution is, we feel perplexed. It is all quite humbling. We all need to have our positive face restored after conflict, to feel that we are still good people, are still admired and respected. Image repair requires the skill of acknowledgment.

Acknowledgment means honouring and saying the positive things we see in the other person and in the actions they take. It *affirms* the goodness and worth of our conflict partner. Conflict resolution should feel affirmative, not punitive, and leave people with a positive motivation for change. Human dignity is precious. Repairing each other's self-image and worth after a conflict gives us our dignity back in each other's eyes. We shouldn't let people walk away thinking we look down on them. This can easily backfire on us later.

Here are some examples of things we can say to repair our conflict partner's image, heal any hurts, and restore goodwill:

- Thank you for being so patient and gracious.
- I respect your working on this with me.
- You are brave and courageous to do this with me.
- I feel closer to you now.

118

- You have been a teacher for me. Thank you.
- I could not have resolved this issue without you.
- I value your honesty and openness.
- My heart is open to you now. Thank you.
- You are powerful. I respect you.
- I wish you all the best and honour your decision.
- You are a wonderful person and I am lucky to know you.
- I value who you are.
- I acknowledge you for being patient and sincere.

The role of forgiveness in conflict

We can hardly talk about making up without mentioning forgiveness. Forgiveness happens when we completely understand how and why things happened the way they did. Then we can forgive, even if what happened hurt us deeply.

Forgiveness is necessary to allow others back into our hearts and unburden our own. But forgiveness, as Buddhist monk Thich Nhat Hanh says, while necessary, cannot be forced. Nor can we use forgiveness as a way to ignore problems in our relationships. We arrive at true forgiveness when we have looked deeply into the matter at hand and have come to *understand* each other. Forgiveness flows naturally from this understanding. How do we find this understanding? Thich Nhat Hanh suggests it is found by *looking deeply*.

We may arrive at this deep level of understanding at the end of a conflict, or it may take more time to really understand and forgive someone. If it is a small matter, it may take five minutes. If the conflict was serious and important, it may take much longer. We can only forgive someone when we are ready. We can't offer it until we have it.

When our opponent apologises to us, we can accept the apology without forgiving them. We simply need to say, 'Thank you'. Chapter 10, Inner Conflict, discusses how we can learn to forgive ourselves and others.

Acknowledging and celebrating

It is important to notice when a conflict gets resolved. Many people don't notice when they have reached resolution, and they keep conflicting when it is time to stop and make up. When the mood has improved and things are beginning to sort themselves out, we can acknowledge this shift in atmosphere. We can say, 'I feel better now. Don't you?'

Noticing and acknowledging when the mood improves increases the healing effects of conflict resolution. When the resolution phase commences, the tension begins to dissolve and the two sides start moving toward each other again. The atmosphere feels more relaxed, warm, connected and hopeful. This is the healing time. We should enjoy and embrace it, bathe in its energy. We can say, 'Things feel different now, the mood is warmer, softer, more open. I feel closer to you! We got somewhere. Yeah!'

When we successfully make up, we should both feel that our self-image as worthy people is restored. We should feel a lessening of tensions. We should feel gratified. We might even feel like celebrating, especially if we were able to find a satisfying resolution together, for that is the joy of completion. It is time to shake hands, slap each other on the back, and go grab that beer. Whatever feels festive and fun.

Exercise: Practise making up

1. Think of a conflict or issue you have with someone.
2. Imagine the conflict is drawing to an end for now. How would you make up? For what would you apologise? How would you repair the other person's self-image? What would you say?
3. Imagine saying these things. What effect does it have? How do you feel afterwards?

Thoughts to hold

- Making up reduces tension and locks in the resolution.
- Making up often requires apologising or repairing the other person's self-image.
- Apology must be heartfelt and unequivocal. It is a gift. Let them receive it.
- We repair the other's self-image by acknowledging the positive things about them.
- Making up creates goodwill, trust and hope for the future of the relationship.

Part Two

What's Holding You Back?

7 Nonverbal Communication

*Why do we invest all our skills and resources in a contest
for armed superiority which can never be attained for long
enough to make it worth having, rather than in an effort
to find a* modus vivendi *with our antagonist – that is to
say, a way of living, not dying?*

Barbara Tuchman, *The March of Folly – From Troy to Vietnam*

During all communication, including conflict, we emit
nonverbal signals through unconscious behaviours such as our
body language and tones of voice. Some say that this nonverbal communication sends an even more powerful message
than our spoken words. For instance, if I say, 'I'd like to spend
time with you', but my body is turned away from you, you
may feel unsure of my sincerity. However, many of us have
been taught to ignore nonverbal behaviour, and certainly to
avoid acknowledging it. Pointing out when someone's body
language doesn't match their words may indeed cause an
embarrassed or defensive reaction. So we may disregard this
crucial information and plunge ahead despite our intuitive
misgivings, only to be sadly disappointed when things don't
work out.

We can learn to pay attention to what people do, as well as
what they say. This information about 'their side' can be a
wonderful aid in conflict resolution.

Escalation and de-escalation: Flash points and cool-downs

To keep things simple, there are really only two types of body language that you need to know for conflict resolution: escalation and de-escalation.

To *escalate* means to increase in volume or intensity, to make things bigger or louder. A conflict is *escalating* when it is getting more intense, more conflictive, more polarised. The tension level is rising. When people escalate in conflict, they are taking their own side more strongly and vigorously. The conflict is heating up. Sometimes it is appropriate to escalate to express our side effectively. It can take some assertion to express our needs and wants, thoughts and feelings.

People escalate for many reasons, the primary one being that they don't feel heard. If we don't feel heard, we tend to express ourselves ever more loudly until we do feel heard, until we receive an apology, or until 'justice' is served. We also escalate when we feel attacked or unfairly criticised or feel the need to defend or protect ourselves.

Nothing drives people crazier than not being heard. When we don't feel heard we try even harder to influence the other side, to *make* them understand. It is not necessarily a conscious process but rather a spontaneous expression of frustration, anger or excitement. This escalation may be expressed verbally by the marshalling of facts and hard data or by more aggressive moves such as cutting the other person off while they are speaking. Or it may manifest itself through nonverbal behaviours such as raised voice tones, yelling, glaring, standing up, moving forward aggressively or clenching fists.

De-escalation is the reverse process. To de-escalate is to

decrease in size, volume, or intensity. A conflict is *de-escalating* when it is getting less tense, less polarised, less threatening, less conflictive. When people de-escalate in conflict, they relax their position and are able to connect with the other side more readily. There is more understanding and openness. We de-escalate a conflict whenever we take the other side or the neutral side. When resolution is reached, people also de-escalate. In fact, the goal of resolution is to de-escalate the tension by addressing it and working through it.

The primary reason people de-escalate is that they feel heard. If we have been hurt but feel 'heard', we will feel less need to continue expressing our hurt and anger. Nothing eases people like being heard. When we feel heard we can relax our efforts to influence the other side. We can let go of our control. De-escalating is not necessarily a conscious process but rather a spontaneous response to feeling heard and understood. De-escalation can be manifested as softened voice tones, smiling, slowing down, nodding, and making affirmative comments to the other side. It is also expressed through physical signals such as leaning back, stretching muscles, sighing, laughing, dropping our shoulders or releasing clenched fists.

Escalation and de-escalation are typically communicated not with words but through body language, facial expression and voice tone. We rarely say, 'OK, I'm escalating now!' We just get red in the face and talk louder. Conversely, we don't tend to say, 'Now I'm relaxing and de-escalating', we just sit back and drop our shoulders.

Of course, words also signal our intentions. We show that we are intensifying the conflict by verbally taking our own side more strongly. We show that we are de-intensifying the conflict by taking the other side and offering understanding. If I say, 'I'm furious with you!' that shows that I am intensifying the conflict. I am escalating. You then think, 'Oh no, now I'm in trouble'. If, on the other hand, I say, 'I really see your point of view', that shows that I am de-intensifying the conflict by taking the other side. I am de-escalating. I am not opposing you. You think, 'Great, she understands me'.

Some research suggests that men tend to escalate more quickly than women. Daniel Goldman, author of *Emotional Intelligence*, writes that men are prone to emotional flooding; that is, they have a lower threshold for tolerating emotion before they begin to flood with adrenaline and feel out of control. Men's apparent distance and coolness may be a way to stay in control and stop themselves from flooding. They may avoid emotional topics because they wish to avoid situations where they might experience unpleasant emotional escalation.

According to Goldman, women experience emotions intensely, but they are well equipped to do so. They can often experience deep emotion without losing control, flooding or escalating. Women's strong need for bonding and affiliation with others also helps them to not over-escalate.

American psychologist Shelley Taylor and her colleagues have recently released groundbreaking research which suggests women respond to stress in more complex ways than do men. In addition to the well-known flight or fight response, women appear to have another behavioural response, called the 'tend and befriend' response, initiated by the release of the brain chemical oxytocin. The 'tend and befriend' model suggests that when women feel stressed, they'll often reach out to other women to calm themselves or tend to their children. This and Goldman's research on emotional intelligence has important implications for how men and women deal with conflict. Expect to read more about this very interesting research in the coming years.

Signs of escalation
- disagreeing
- feeling tense and hot
- feeling anger or self-righteousness
- feeling excitement, involvement, energy
- wanting to hurt or punish the other side
- yelling
- making verbal threats
- being insulting, rude or hurtful
- standing up or pacing restlessly
- gritting teeth, clenching fists, glaring, raising voice
- thinking you're right

Signs of de-escalation
- genuinely listening to the other side
- pausing or resting
- relaxing, lying down, leaning back
- lowering of voice
- feeling warmth, love, compassion for the other side
- humour or laughing
- breathing freely
- feeling calmer
- smiling and nodding
- agreeing

When words and bodies don't match

Our body language frames our verbal communication and gives the listener clues about how to interpret our worded message. For instance, if I say, 'I'm really furious with you', but I look down and my voice is low and unsure, the listener might think, 'Well, she says she's angry but she doesn't look it. She looks shy or embarrassed. What's going on with her?' On the other hand, if I say, 'I can see your point of view', but I am glaring or sounding harsh or sarcastic, this is also confusing. The listener may think, 'She says she understands me, but she looks angry. I'm afraid of her. I don't trust her no matter what she says.'

We may not be aware of escalating or de-escalating because so much of our communication is unconscious. This can make conflict complex and frustrating. We say one thing but do another. (One popular example is the infamous 'Fine!') Furthermore, we don't notice that this is happening and so we keep going round and round in circles. People's words hypnotise our conscious mind, but our body reacts to their whole-body communication.

Thriller movies capitalise on this split between words and behaviour. We know someone is creepy in a movie when their words do not match their body language. The audience sees this and it nearly drives us to despair when the heroine is oblivious to the danger. 'Wake up!' we want to yell. 'Can't you see he's lying?'

Body language is often perceived on an unconscious level, so it takes a little extra effort to notice it. It is surprisingly obvious when pointed out to us. We just have to look for it. When we step out of a conflict and look at it from the neutral point of view, we often become aware of the body language.

Emails and other non-visual communication

Sometimes we can't see the other person because we're communicating via email or fax. We can only see the written word. Sometimes we can only hear the person, for example, when we're on the phone. These non-visual communication mediums present special communication challenges and if not handled well can lead to unintended conflicts and misunderstandings.

Email in particular can lead to conflict and ill will as people often feel slighted when they receive an email they perceive to be brusque, rude or demanding. Usually the email writer doesn't intend this, they just haven't considered the impact of their email upon the reader. But because the reader can't see or hear us, they are entirely dependent on the written word for meaning, tone and nuance. They can't see the twinkle in our eye or our wry smile, they can't hear our warm tone of voice or dry sense of humour. That's why it's crucial to be warm and courteous with email – always. In the absence of these obvious written signals, people fill in the blanks and often imagine the worst. As email is so widely used today, it's important to use it carefully and thoughtfully to promote positive relationships with others.

Hot spot: Temperatures rising

There is a moment when a conflict is escalating and suddenly reaches a kind of crescendo or a flash point. My conflict resolution mentor once did a great demonstration of escalation. He and his partner Amy pretended to have a fight, but instead of using words they used gibberish, nonsense sounds. They squawked and squealed at each other, sometimes raising their voices quite high. Then they would drop their voices for a few seconds into grumbles, returning a few moments later to high-pitched squawking. Isn't this how most conflicts look? A series of loud squawks and low grumbles?

The particularly loud or tense squawking moments, we call Hot Spots. Normally, we retreat quickly from these spots, because they are too hot to handle and we don't know what to do with them. The conflict feels like it is 'getting out of control'. We get scared of the intensity.

It is important for us to notice hot spots because they tell us that the conflict is escalating. It is escalating because one or both people do not feel heard and they are beginning to use greater force to get their message across. If the conflict continues this way unchecked, it is likely to continue until hurtful and damaging things get said. This is when people try to topple the other side with insults and put-downs. If that doesn't work, one party walks off or a physical fight may ensue.

Hot spots are full of energy and tension. They are highly charged emotional moments. This is when we 'lose it' and say all manner of exaggerated things. Sometimes these can be great moments of truth, when our real feelings or thoughts finally pop out, but usually it is just a lot of hot air and venting of spleen.

Normally when people get this heated in a conflict, it is helpful to ask them to step back from the conflict and look at how they are feeling. Why are they so angry, what is behind their need to shout down the other side? Most people will say that they are getting heated because they feel frustrated, wronged or not heard. We can diffuse this situation by listening to their feelings. Showing your understanding allows the other side to relax and de-escalate. We know this instinctively.

The exception to this rule is when someone is addicted to anger or stuck in a pattern of behaving abusively toward others. Some people are 'escalators'. They escalate quickly and frequently over every little issue. Escalators use anger to control others and avoid deeper discussion. This is a separate issue needing professional help. Typically these people are recreating the abusive drama of childhood, when they were on the receiving end of this anger. These people need to learn about what motivates their behaviour and how they can heal themselves. They need to learn that conflict is not an excuse for mistreating others. The presence of alcohol greatly increases the likelihood that things will escalate out of control. Never attempt conflict resolution when either party has been drinking, even a little.

Some women err on the side of not escalating enough. They have trouble expressing themselves adequately, or feel too shy or afraid to say what they think. Other women are volcanoes who use force or anger to get heard and to get their way. These women need to learn that they can get heard without over-escalating. It is usually wiser to approach tension with gentleness and respect for one another, with each side listening deeply and also expressing their own side effectively and assertively.

Anger: The common escalator

Anger is the most common reason for escalating. We all get angry at times. Anger is an emotional response to being hurt or frustrated. It also arises when we want to change things. It is normal to have occasional grievances and to feel anger.

Getting clear about our anger and expressing it respectfully keeps our communication functional and effective. Failure to do so can result in the build up of resentment. Having a backlog of unresolved anger can result in the tendency to explode abusively when we are triggered by a minor incident, creating havoc.

On the other hand, inhibitions about getting angry can make it hard to take our own side or escalate our position effectively. A little anger can really help us get our point across. People who condemn all expressions of anger are often in fact fearful of their own repressed aggression. They can accept everything but anger! While we don't want to create unnecessary conflict with a belligerent attitude, we all may benefit from a little dose of extra assertiveness at times to get us to participate in productive conflict in the first place. The conversation that ensues may be crucial for connecting with each other and discovering solutions to our shared problems. On the other hand, using anger as a weapon is ultimately destructive. Anger doesn't create resolutions. Listening and learning does.

Conflict resolution is helpful because it provides a safe arena in which to express our anger openly and directly. Oddly enough, in our culture nagging, complaining, avoidance, sarcasm, criticism, withdrawal and other dirty fighting tactics are often regarded as more acceptable than direct expressions of anger or concern. This may be because they are indirect and therefore less confrontational. When someone expresses anger openly, we take note, whether we agree with them or not. The clearer, cleaner and more direct we are, the more effective our communication will be.

When people feel free and safe to express themselves, knowing they will be heard, a lot of the hysterics, antics, drama and desperation evaporate. We stop playing games. We become respectful. We stop exaggerating our feelings and using dirty fighting tactics. The drama stops and real communication begins. We begin to connect as collaborators in problem solving.

Female anger

Women more than men tend to have the habit of holding back their angry feelings for long stretches of time and then expressing them in one giant blast, much to the shock of partners and friends. Where did that come from, others think? Many men say they fear women's anger and don't understand it. It often seems unbalanced and out of proportion to events.

On the other side, many women say they have a lot to be angry about. For instance, women complain about feeling unheard by male partners and are frustrated with them as a result. They want the empathy and understanding they receive from female friends. When this isn't forthcoming from a man, they react negatively. Unfortunately being angry with others rarely changes them. It usually frightens them, makes them angry in return or shuts them down emotionally. Most people dislike being on the receiving end of anger and will resist it.

Tiredness, lack of emotional support, illness and premenstrual tension can all act as triggers for a woman to lose it. The pressure of daily life builds up and suddenly overrides the still strong social message that women shouldn't get angry and should put others' needs before their own. It's easy to see why a woman might suddenly explode from time to time. The lid has got to come off the pressure cooker sometime! If I feel particularly upset or angry, I try to sort out my feelings before sitting down to discuss a conflict. Otherwise I won't be able to think straight. Usually I talk it out with a trusted friend who knows how to help me. This reduces my emotional pressure, clears my head and allows me to explore the root of my anger. What is my anger telling me? What do I want? Then I'm ready for the conflict discussion. Anger can be a powerful motivator and force for change. Use it to take positive action in your life, not to crush others.

If you find yourself losing emotional control during a conflict situation, stop talking for a moment and breathe deeply. Look at the situation from the neutral side to see why you're getting so upset. When you know, express your feelings calmly and clearly. For more ideas on how on to stay focused and centred during a conflict, read Chapter 9, Developing Clarity. If you do lose it with someone, always apologise afterwards, even if they are technically in the wrong. I barked at someone once for not helping me lift a heavy object. They still didn't help! I apologised afterwards for my outburst and discovered that they didn't help because of a back injury. We get on famously now, which would not be the case without my apology.

One way to reduce the likelihood of losing your temper with others is to feel more confident about taking your own side regularly and getting more of what you want in life. Self-sacrifice and silent suffering can lead to a mountain of resentment, which needs only a small trigger to cause a landslide. While I'm not suggesting that women shouldn't express their anger, losing emotional control rarely helps the conflict resolution process and mostly worsens it. If you're experiencing a conflict where there's too much anger and pain for you to deal with comfortably, get help from a counsellor or mediator.

Sometimes the expression of anger and pain is important for resolution. This is particularly true for deeper reconciliation processes requiring trained mediators, such as victim–offender reconciliation processes, highly emotive and divisive community issues, and heavily polarised political situations. These scenarios often require the sharing of difficult emotion and stories to promote connection between sides and allow reconciliation and resolution to occur.

Finally, I have noticed that confident and assertive people rarely get angry. They seem less easily threatened, have good emotional control, are tolerant and considerate and know how to draw the line without blasting the other side into oblivion. You can be assertive and get your point across without using anger or being a doormat.

Healthy feminine aggression: The energy to pursue our needs

Normal healthy aggression is the energy we need to get up each morning and pursue our goals in life. Women are increasingly reaching out and pursuing development in all areas of life. As we do so, we learn to honour and express our healthy feminine aggression. We need a certain amount of aggression to take our own side in conflict and in life. This is really our vitality, our life force, that forward-moving energy we need to take responsibility for our welfare and happiness and to take positive action on our own behalf. We may feel dissatisfied at things in our lives but it takes the mobilisation of our energy to do something about it. It is that extra push that enables us to take charge of our lives, to insist on making time to connect with the important people in our lives, to take our own side, and to ensure that tensions are resolved.

Tension spotting

Tension is part of life. It alerts us when things need attention or problems need solving, and when we need to connect more deeply with the people in our lives. So it is important to notice and acknowledge when tension arises, or when it dissolves, whether things get tenser or more relaxed. For instance, when it feels tense, we can say, 'It feels a little tense. What shall we do? Shall we focus on it for a while? What's up? Let's talk.'

Here is a tension barometer to help identify the state of tension in the conflict:

High tension: Not speaking to each other or yelling hostilities at each other.

Mild tension: Angry or moody but able to tell partner about it.

Healthy tension: Interacting happily, playful banter, good energy flow and connection.

Absence of tension: Harmonious atmosphere, calm, healing and loving communication.

Suppressed tension: Dull, dead atmosphere, predictable routine communication.

The warmth of connection: Keeping an even heat

By gently working through the tensions in our lives, we build peace. Instead of leaving a dark cloud of tension between us, we can decide to sit down and work through the tension in a safe, organised space. We reveal whatever thoughts, emotions, opinions, or stories we feel are relevant to the current tension. Conflict and tension are simply indicators that connection and conversation need to happen.

It is important to realise that conflict normally goes through a cycle of escalation and de-escalation as an issue gets worked out. Conflict resolution works best when there is a gentle heat that keeps things moving along. The trick is to provide sufficient escalation to keep the dialogue gently simmering, but not so much as to start a fire. There needs to be enough de-escalation to allow people to rest and absorb the information, but not so much that it snuffs out the dialogue through lack of energy or interest.

Many people have either a too-hot style, which blows things sky-high, or a too-cool style, which dampens dialogue until it fizzles. One way to keep an even heat is to be honest and real. This keeps things alive. But be careful not to be overly critical or judgmental! That causes things to escalate unpleasantly.

You decide on the heat level

By keeping a neutral eye on the conflict, you can de-escalate things when they are getting too hot. You can take a break, make a joke, or listen to the other side sincerely. Similarly, you can inject a little energy into the proceedings when it looks like it is about to fizzle by taking your side more convincingly or encouraging the other side to express themselves more fully. Knowing how to control the temperature of a conflict gives you more control and a sense of safety.

Story: An example of escalation and de-escalation

Michael and Patricia are planning an upcoming trip to Melbourne to visit Patricia's parents. It is the first time they have visited her parents together and the trip holds much significance, especially for her. Michael has ambivalent feelings about the trip. Here is how they dealt with some of the underlying issues.

Round one

Patricia: 'Well, what's with you?' *(Communicates her awareness of tension in the relationship.)*

Michael: 'I've been thinking about the trip. I don't know if I want to go to Melbourne to see your family.' *(Escalates: Takes his own side.)*

Patricia: 'But the tickets are booked!' *(Escalates: Reacts strongly by taking her own side.)*

Michael: 'I don't want to spend nine days with your family. It's too long!' *(Escalates: Takes his own side.)*

Patricia: 'That's not long! I only see them every few years.' *(Escalates: Takes her own side.)*

Michael: 'But we haven't even planned what we're going to do for those nine days!' *(Escalates: Takes his own side.)*

Patricia: 'We'll just wing it, honey. We can do whatever we like.' *(De-escalates: Smiles, uses a soft voice, tries to be pleasant but is not listening to Michael's complaint.)*

Michael: 'I don't feel you've considered me in this trip.' *(Escalates:*

Takes his own side and ignores Patricia's attempt to de-escalate.)

Patricia: 'Look, we'll just figure it out when we get there, okay!' *(Escalates: Takes her own side. Is irritated that her de-escalation attempt failed.)*

Michael: 'Why not now?' *(Continues to take his own side.)*

Patricia: 'To be honest, I just haven't thought about it yet.' *(De-escalates: Tone is low and unsure.)*

Michael 'Precisely.' *(Escalates: Tone is superior.)*

Patricia: 'Oh, screw you!' *(Escalates.)*

End of round one.

Analysis

Michael expresses concern about the upcoming trip to Melbourne. Patricia tries to deflect this but does not do so effectively. She tries to de-escalate the conflict by being sweet ('We'll just wing it, honey,') but this fails. She doesn't know how to deal with Michael's complaint effectively. Michael also takes his side ineffectively. He complains but he doesn't tell Patricia what is really bothering him.

Round two

Patricia: 'Let's talk. How can I help?' *(De-escalates: Offers to listen.)*

Michael: 'I feel like you're not considering me in this trip. You haven't talked to me about it, except to make dates for the flight.' *(Escalates: Continues taking his own side.)*

Patricia: 'Michael, I need your support on this trip. I'm taking you to meet my parents. You and I have been together for a year and they haven't even met you. They want to meet you. This is really important for me.' *(Escalates: Takes her side. However, the conversation is beginning to open and deepen.)*

Michael: 'I didn't know this trip was so important to you. You haven't talked about it. You're always so busy.' *(Escalates but is beginning to soften.)*

Patricia: 'You're right. I'm sorry about that.' *(De-escalates: Apologises.)*

Michael: 'I just don't feel together with you on this trip.' *(Continues to take his side but his tone is vulnerable as the emotional core of his side emerges.)*

Patricia: 'Michael, can't you just co-operate with me!' *(Escalates again: Her tone is impatient. Misses his emerging need.)*

Michael: 'I'm just saying what I think!' *(Escalates: He is upset that she is unable to hear him.)*

Patricia: 'Do what you want then!' *(Escalates: Hostile voice tone.)*

End of round two.

Analysis

The conflict is cycling. Michael has trouble expressing his needs directly and complains and criticises instead. He doesn't see that this is not an effective way to get his needs met. Patricia fails to see that Michael is indirect with his needs and so she doesn't address it. She just blows up. Neither of them has an overview of what is happening. What would you suggest as the neutral party? What do you see?

Round three

Patricia: 'I'm bothered by your attitude, Michael. You're criticising me and acting neglected. I would prefer it if you just said what you wanted.' *(Escalates: Challenges Michael's behaviour and takes her own side.)*

Michael: 'I am acting childishly. I'm sorry. It's just that I feel I'm only here to pay for the tickets and be shown off.' *(De-escalates by apologising. Then escalates by continuing to take his side.)*

Patricia: 'I see. Like I'm the one controlling this trip. Like we're not doing this together. Is that right?' *(De-escalates by taking his side.)*

Michael: 'Yes. I want to plan this trip with you. I don't want to "wing" it.' *(De-escalates by responding positively to Patricia's support.)*

Patricia: 'You're right. I was just planning the trip in my head without discussing it. And you're right – I have been busy. Okay, let's sit down and do it together. I want us to be together in this.' *(De-escalates by taking Michael's side.)*

Michael: 'Thank you. I'm sorry about being moody. That isn't fair to you. You don't deserve that. I'm grateful to you for listening.' *(De-escalates: Apologises and repairs Patricia's image. Makes up.)*

Resolution

Patricia and Michael sit down to discuss the trip. They also discuss their feelings about the conflict. Michael sees how he complains and criticises instead of saying what he wants. Patricia sees her tendency to feel guilty and burdened instead of tackling issues head-on, such as confronting Michael's indirect expression of his needs. But Patricia finally broke the unproductive cycling by confronting Michael's conflict tactics. Michael was then able to express his needs directly and Patricia was able to hear and respond to those needs. Patricia also saw where Michael was right – that in her anxiety about visiting her parents she had become controlling about the trip.

We see from this example that escalation and de-escalation can be either productive or unproductive. We can escalate in a positive manner by being assertive and honest, or we can escalate in a negative manner by being sarcastic and defensive. Similarly, we can de-escalate in a positive manner by listening and reaching out, or we can de-escalate in a negative manner by acting appeasing or timid.

Listening: The best de-escalator

Listening is the most important ingredient in de-escalating tension and resolving conflict. People quickly reach their boiling point when they feel their conflict partner is not listening to or understanding them. This is a very human response to not being heard. It can turn even the most rational, calm person into a ranting maniac. The same thing happens if we twist or distort the meaning of someone's words. This is because our communication is our primary means of connecting with the outer world. To have our communication ignored or misunderstood is frustrating. See Chapter 4, Take the Other Side, for more about listening.

Story: Triangle tensions

Jess was a bright engaging woman in her fifties who had a successful career as a town planner. She'd been single for eight years but now felt ready for a relationship. One day she met Michael, a man she felt she could fall in love with. Trouble was, her flatmate and friend, Selena, felt the same way! A classic triangle situation was beginning to develop between Jess, Selena and Michael.

Jess decided to ask Michael to lunch, though aware that Michael had already made contact with Selena to ask her out. Selena had declined the invitation from Michael because she wanted Jess to have an opportunity to pursue her feelings for Michael. After all, it had been eight years since Jess had dated! Selena decided to sacrifice her own feelings for Michael because she wanted to support Jess, her closest friend in the world. However, Selena's decision to take Jess's side and not her own in a spirit of sisterly altruism was to rebound on her later, with destructive results.

Michael arrived for lunch on a Sunday, at Jess's invitation, and all seemed to be going well until Selena arrived home. Jess saw Michael and Selena talking together, and it looked more than friendly. Was Selena flirting with Michael? How could she? How could he?

Jess felt betrayed by Selena but said nothing for two days. Finally, unable to contain her feelings anymore, she told Selena she felt hurt and betrayed by her. Bad timing! That week, Selena was in the middle of her final law exams and was in a highly stressed and frazzled condition. Selena felt attacked and unsupported during her exam week. They had a heated exchange in which Selena said she felt Jess was thoughtless and selfish to bring up the Michael issue during her exam week. She yelled at Jess and seemed highly emotional and angry.

Jess had to think fast. Should she defend herself? Yell back? Explain her actions? Accuse Selena of sliding off the issue of flirting with Michael after saying she'd step aside for Jess?

Fortunately, Jess was able to use the conflict resolution skills I describe in this book. She recognised that Selena was highly escalated; angry, emotional, stressed out and not being entirely logical. She knew she would be unable to have a sensible conversation with Selena while she was so emotionally charged. To escalate things further by being adversarial could possibly damage their relationship even more. She decided to de-escalate the situation. How did she do this?

She listened.

She heard Selena out.

She attempted to see where Selena's complaints were true.

She allowed Selena to feel heard.

She spoke slowly, calmly and softly.

Selena calmed down once she saw that Jess was listening and not retaliating in kind. The tension went out of Selena's body, her shoulders dropped and her voice became quieter. She was de-escalating.

Now they could talk.

Jess admitted she had unthinkingly chosen a difficult time to raise this issue but hadn't meant it maliciously. Most difficult of all to admit, Jess had deliberately overlooked the fact that Michael had contacted Selena first, in her rush to snare Michael. Although Selena had said she'd step aside while Jess pursued Michael, Jess now saw that Selena could not build a barricade around her heart, just to please her. Jess also saw that her quest for Michael was going to be unsuccessful. She would support Selena to pursue Michael herself, if that was what she wanted to do.

Selena was grateful for Jess's understanding and acknowledgment of her contribution to the conflict. She apologised for blowing up at Jess. They continued to talk through the situation over the next few weeks, having realised that their relationship was strong enough to handle the truth.

How was Jess able to de-escalate the situation and take Selena's side even when she herself felt so hurt, disappointed, betrayed and attacked?

First, she recognised the signs of escalation and worked to de-escalate the conflict effectively in the moment.

Second, Jess had been able to search inside herself and discover that resolving the conflict could only be done by aligning her own behaviour with her deepest value: freedom. She wanted Selena to be free to follow her heart, just as she wished to be free to follow hers. If Michael preferred Selena to her, and Selena wished to reciprocate, than that was life and she would accept it. A friendship based on freedom to follow one's heart was the kind of friendship she wanted with Selena. She was big enough for that. She was a wise and mature woman who could resolve complex and painful issues with her most intimate female friends.

Selena, for her part, was able to take Jess's side more completely once she had finished her exams. Selena had been deeply touched by Jess's ability to give Selena the freedom to follow her heart, even if it meant disappointment for Jess.

And how did the story end? Jess got over her attraction to Michael and can now see he wasn't right for her. Selena is slowly getting to know Michael but is unsure of what will develop. Both women have agreed that their fears about finding a man created an unspoken competition between them over Michael. But most importantly, the values of truth and freedom have been upheld and reinforced in Jess and Selena's friendship.

Our values can help us de-escalate conflict.

Our values can help us resolve conflict.

Humour: The fun de-escalator

Along with listening, humour is a great de-escalator. We all need comic relief, especially during conflict, which can be very serious. Humour relieves tension. It releases pent-up energies and allows people to gain perspective.

The sudden urge to laugh is a spontaneous de-escalation response. Sometimes it happens when people are doing the Big Volcano Blast. Once I had a conflict with a friend. He got so mad he grabbed his telephone and started waving it in the air. The cord wrapped itself around his arm, entangling him hopelessly. He got so frustrated with it, he finally flung it to the floor and stormed upstairs. It was priceless, pure Three Stooges. I couldn't hold back my laughter. My friend, being a good sport, returned several minutes later grinning sheepishly and apologised for his insane outburst. Being able to laugh is a wonderful attribute. Humour helps us accept those moments when one or both of us simply need to go nuts and let off steam. We all need to have a fit from time to time.

Laughing is not always an effective de-escalator. Nervous laughter can be an expression of fear that things could get heavy. Sarcastic laughter is actually a put-down, often meant to humiliate or intimidate.

Fear: The self-protective de-escalator

Listening and laughing are positive ways to de-escalate a conflict, if used judiciously. Fear is another very important de-escalation signal. If we experience fear in a conflict, there may be something to be afraid of – perhaps there is the potential for something hurtful to be said or done. There are at least three reasons we may experience fear in conflict.

1. We may fear the other side due to past experiences of him or her being verbally or physically abusive. Our fear of the other side is a realistic fear based on our recent experience. If we are afraid to conflict because of a real abuse of some kind, we need to say so. Then we need to spend some serious time reflecting on why we are in a relationship in which we can't conflict safely. *It is imperative to our health that we feel free to discuss our differences with those close to us.* That is how trust works – through the open sharing of ourselves without fear of harm. If our conflict partner refuses to address tensions in a fair way, the relationship has a short life span. It can't grow. We can't risk real intimacy, which means trusting each other enough to be vulnerable.

2. We may fear the other side because *someone else* was abusive or hurtful to us in the past, such as a parent, caregiver or teacher. In this case, our fear is a reactive fear rooted in the past. Learning conflict resolution skills can assist us in overcoming past fears and help us feel more confident in the present. Therapy, coaching, counselling and martial arts training can also help us overcome fear of conflict caused by negative experiences in the past.

3. We may fear conflict in general and the discomfort of a possible rupture in the relationship. This is an understandable fear, especially for women. Women often de-escalate, even when their side is important to them, because they are afraid of conflict itself. They can act submissively to prevent any rupture in the relationship. If we notice that we have a tendency to act submissively during a conflict, we can say,

'I'm nervous about having a conflict with you', or 'I have feelings about this issue but I don't want anyone to get hurt.' Expressing our fear is a powerful act. It helps establish safety, which is a vital part of the work. We can use our fear to establish the ground rules. We need to let the other side know what works for us and what doesn't, what we can tolerate and what we cannot. We should tell the other side what we need in order to be able to enter the discussion. Used this way, fear becomes our ally. This fear of conflict itself is discussed extensively in Chapter 8, Fear of Conflict. Feeling confident of our conflict resolution skills can help us to deal with conflict in ways that do not harm relationship.

The body language of fear

Fear is expressed through signals such as looking down or away, speaking timidly, smiling weakly, becoming inarticulate, overly agreeing, never disagreeing, being silent, turning away with the body, raised shoulders, sweating, not breathing, breathing shallowly and nervous laughing. Expressing our fear verbally can make the atmosphere safer because it reminds everyone to exercise care and caution. We can say, 'I feel nervous. Let's be sensitive.' It is wise to listen to our fear and never to push it aside. Acting tough when we are afraid creates a mixed message, which can lead to misunderstanding.

Exercise: Tracking your body in conflict

This exercise will help you notice when you are escalating or de-escalating in a conflict situation by becoming aware of your body language. It trains you to become aware of the escalation and de-escalation signals that are often nonverbal, such as voice tone, facial expressions, gestures and movements.

1. Choose a conflict that is bothering you. Let it play out in your mind. Imagine or visualise both sides taking their own side.

2. Ask yourself, 'What is my body doing? How do I feel? Am I becoming tenser or more relaxed?' These are good questions to keep asking yourself throughout a conflict.

3. Take note of your body language. For example, you might notice that your shoulders are tense and that your body is escalating. This could mean that you need to take your own side more effectively. What is it that you are not saying? Conversely, you might notice that you want to lean back and take it easy, that your body is de-escalating. Now you could say, 'I feel open to what you have to say'.

4. Now look at the other person in your imagination. What does his or her nonverbal behaviour tell you? Do they look tense? Are they wanting to escalate their position? Do they look relaxed or open? Do they look fearful or afraid to conflict? Do their words match their body language?

5. Use your awareness of their body language to help out. If they look tense, ask them to speak up. Say, 'I sense you need to say more'. If they look more relaxed or are sitting back, acknowledge their de-escalation. Say, 'You seem more relaxed right now. Is that right?'

7. How does having an awareness of body language help you in the conflict?

Thoughts to hold

- Escalation is when a conflict increases in intensity.
- De-escalation is when a conflict decreases in intensity.
- Watch people's body language, don't just listen to what they say. Are they tensing or relaxing?
- You need to escalate a little to take your own side effectively.
- Anger escalates conflict, so express anger with care.
- Listening to the other side helps to de-escalate tension.
- Humour is a good way to de-escalate tension.
- Our fear can help us create safety in conflict. We can use our fear to create ground rules.

8 Fear of Conflict

The moment we begin to fear the opinions of others and hesitate to tell the truth that is in us, and from motives of policy are silent when we should speak, the divine floods of light and life flow no longer into our souls . . . Every truth we see is ours to give the world, not to keep to ourselves alone, for in doing so we cheat humanity out of their right and check our own development.

Elizabeth Stanton Cady

I have taught conflict resolution to groups dealing with issues as complex and demanding as sexism and racism. I did my doctoral dissertation on conflict resolution. You'd think by now I'd be comfortable with conflict, able to face adversaries with calm and resolve. But in fact I felt compelled to understand the dynamics of conflict and to master conflict resolution tools precisely because I was afraid of conflict.

My conflict resolution mentor once said to me that the best conflict mediators are people who hate conflict. 'That's me!' I thought. People who hate conflict are often very sensitive to the feelings of others in conflict and as a result can be gifted at facilitating communication between conflicting parties. I also taught myself to swim as an adult because I could no longer stand my fear of water. In learning to swim I used patience and self-love to work through my fear of putting my face directly in water. Now I love swimming and have been complimented

153

quite often on my stroke. I used to sit by the pool and watch swimmers glide up and down the pool. I watched each detail of their performance, how they dove, how they stroked, and most importantly for me, how they used their breathing, synchronising breaths with turns of the head. Then I would get in the pool and carefully try to replicate what I had seen. I did the same with conflict. I studied with masters who knew how to conflict effectively and watched them closely, replicating what I saw. Like learning to swim and conquering my fear of water, learning to deal with conflict has been a path of self-development for me, as it can be for you.

I now see that some of the things we are most afraid of are actually secret talents waiting to be discovered. Now when I teach conflict resolution to women I am overjoyed to watch them grasp the concepts and skills and come to a new appreciation of the role of conflict in their lives. It is thrilling to watch women feel empowered to make use of this very important energy and to learn to use it to create deeper connection with others and make wiser choices for themselves.

Growing up without models for handling conflict

Like many women, I grew up without any models for dealing with conflict. I simply had no real idea about what to do. For instance, as a child, I never wanted to take sides in conflict because I was afraid the person I opposed would be hurt. I didn't know then that I could support both sides. I thought I had to make a choice. Someone had to be right and someone had to be wrong. I instinctively felt that winning or losing a conflict would mean trouble further down the track. Not wanting further trouble, I resisted getting involved. Unfortunately, by refusing to get involved, I would then feel stuck and be unable to resolve issues.

I would sometimes envy girls who could tackle others head-on and defend themselves strongly, who could speak their mind without fearing what others thought of them. But I was also disturbed by the fact that those girls didn't seem to care about the other side. Those girls were feared and not always liked. It was simply not possible for me not to care about the other side. What to do? Was there a way to have my say and also support the other side? Was there a way to resolve conflict safely that didn't damage the relationship, myself or the other person? I lacked a model for handling conflict.

It was only later in life, through my studies of psychology, the peace movement, and conflict resolution, that I found models that allowed me to work through tension in ways that maintained my integrity and strengthened my relationships. I personally think that the topic of conflict resolution should be included in all primary and high school syllabuses.

Why we fear conflict

Our fear of conflict is very human and rooted in several causes. First, our primitive brain activates our fight-or-flight mechanism whenever we are faced with a threatening situation or altercation with another. It can take plenty of self-control to stand still and deal with conflict using our higher faculties when adrenaline is pumping through our system.

Second, abusive encounters in childhood may have created

deep pockets of fear that are triggered in adversarial settings. If conflict in our family of origin led to emotional abuse or physical violence, whenever we see someone angry or upset with us we may expect the worse – to be hurt. In addition, we may have learned from our abusers that we can get our needs met by intimidating others with anger or manipulative behaviour.

Third, we simply have not been taught safe and effective techniques for addressing and resolving conflict. In some households, all conflict is strictly prohibited; in others abusive or dirty fighting tactics are used. In either case, we can't learn healthy conflict techniques if we are never exposed to them. This lack of skills makes our attempts at resolving conflict a rather haphazard and frightening affair.

Fourth, conditioning about our roles as women may have created a deep layer of fear in many of us. Women are encouraged to be receptive caretakers of others, often at the cost of our own needs. We women have traditionally been encouraged to be excessively dependent in our relationships. If we feel our survival is dependent on keeping others happy, this can breed fear of conflict. But how happy and safe can we be if we are not free to express ourselves? Many opportunities for growth and connection are lost. The results are boredom, resentment, insecurity, and a sense of deadness in our lives and our relationships.

Another reason we may fear conflict is because the other side is a dirty fighter who tries to hurt our feelings. We may also fear conflict when there is a power difference between us and the other party. We have less power or rank than the other person and feel it is dangerous or unwise to conflict with him or her. Finally, we may fear conflict because a particular issue is a sore spot for us, which makes us feel nervous or afraid.

Do you know what you fear most about conflict? Here are some common fears women have about conflict. Perhaps you can think of others. Women often fear:

- anger in oneself and others
- not being liked
- being hurt, criticised or wounded
- hurting someone else
- ruining or losing the relationship
- one's own power
- competing
- difference and disagreement
- strong emotion
- dirty fighting tactics being used
- not being able to stand up for oneself
- loss of something we need or value

Female double binds

Many women say they feel apprehension about conflict because they don't feel confident about taking their own side. They have never been encouraged to do so. Instead of learning to express their viewpoint, they have been raised to understand what others need or want of them, to please. For a woman to do otherwise was often viewed as selfish. This puts a woman at a distinct disadvantage in conflict because she does not feel free to represent her own side. Thus she must avoid conflict, as it puts her in an emotional double bind. On the one hand, if she stands up for her position, she breaks the implicit social contract of what it means to be a good woman. On the other hand, if she only supports the other side, she loses by default.

Feminist scholars have also written about women's social training to take care of others, to be good listeners, to apologise quickly, to surrender their position readily, to agree with the other side and strive to please, all to affirm the sense of connection between themselves and others and to acquire acceptance or love. This relationship orientation is a very beautiful aspect of feminine life and not to be criticised, because it is a powerful force for human society, culture and community. However, it can mean that anything that threatens this sense of connection can threaten a woman's sense of self and survival.

In many respects, this relationship orientation may be changing as women gain economic independence and have less need to sacrifice themselves in relationship. The divorce rate is an indication that suppression of conflict is not as prevalent in marriage as it once was. And the majority of divorces are initiated by women.

But despite these changes, it is still true that women view relationship with others as a primary source of identity. When a relationship enters a state of polarisation through conflict, it becomes momentarily de-stabilised. Rather than risk a possible rupture of relationship, women (and men too) may give up their side in order to maintain the sense of connection and harmony. The relationship is actually weakened by this misguided attempt to preserve it. This strategy masks and denies the reality that there are different needs in the relationship.

One of the helpful things about conflict resolution is that it gives both sides a chance to be both assertive *and* supportive, competitive *and* co-operative. You don't have to choose to be one or the other. In fact, resolution is only possible when we express our own side *and* listen to and understand the other. You can be pro-relationship and still have your own viewpoint and needs.

Here is a list of qualities traditionally viewed as feminine. Many of these qualities are deeply loving and very useful for knowing how to take the other side and for being neutral in a conflict, both highly important skills. They can also be useful for cultivating compassion for our own side, including our fears:

- co-operation over competition
- peacemaking
- care taking of others
- compassion
- concern for others' feelings and needs
- selflessness
- patience
- empathy and receptivity

Story: Bully at work

Catherine found herself in a difficult situation at work. Newly recruited, she had been put together with a talented staff member, Adam, to work on a new and innovative product in their advertising company. She greatly admired Adam and wanted to learn from him. As time went by, however, she saw that Adam had traits that concerned her. Adam was outspoken and prone to reacting angrily to management decisions he didn't agree with. Catherine felt somewhat intimated by this angry behaviour, yet she valued his skills and wanted to maintain a positive working relationship with him. What could she do?

One day, Catherine made a decision about the project that Adam disagreed with. Their manager decided to go with Catherine's instinct in this case. Adam became incensed, marched into Catherine's office and accused her of being 'manager's pet'. He stormed out of her office, muttering sarcastically about Catherine's 'instincts'. Catherine sat there feeling stunned and paralysed. Should she confront his behaviour? She went to his office but he had shut the door. She knocked on the door but he didn't answer. Catherine packed her bag and left work, wondering how she could continue to work in an environment that was so volatile.

Catherine needed to face some facts. First, she needed to admit to herself that she was afraid of Adam, afraid of confronting other people's behaviour. Second, she needed help to think about how to approach the problem. We discussed the options available to her. Do nothing – not really an option, as the problem wouldn't go away on its own. Go to human resources and lodge a grievance complaint against Adam under the workplace bullying and harassment legislation. Catherine would have been quite within her rights to do so, but was concerned about taking this step. It would mean irreversible damage to her working relationship with Adam. Few relationships can withstand a legalistic action of this sort. If she pursued this path, she would need to accept that the matter would be out of her hands and she would not be able to engage in conflict resolution. The process would be documented officially, determined by policy, and probably be adversarial. She could also approach her manager. She was entitled to do so but she didn't know the manager well and sensed it would also damage her relationship with Adam. How could she stand up to Adam in an effective manner that would improve their relationship, not damage it? After all, she had no intention of seeking another job.

We prepared for the conversation she needed to have with Adam, using role play. The situation presented Catherine with a steep learning curve and an opportunity to develop as an individual. She would need to move beyond her fear and claim her power to be successful.

That week at work she spoke to Adam in private. She took her own side by saying she had been upset by his behaviour in her office and was requesting that he not behave like that in the future. Adam denied that his behaviour had been a problem and felt justified anger at what he perceived to be a poor project decision on her part. Catherine was prepared for this denial from Adam and carefully stuck to her plan. She didn't become emotional but calmly maintained her side until she felt he was hearing her. She said that she understood that he felt anger but that it wasn't okay for him to express his anger in that manner in the workplace. She was empathic of his feeling but not of his behaviour. Adam continued to resist her side. She then escalated the conflict by letting him know that she considered his behaviour to be workplace bullying. This brought Adam up short. He now realised that this was a most serious conversation.

Catherine had left this inflammatory and serious accusation till last, giving Adam a chance first to take her side, which he had failed to do. Catherine was prepared to raise the stakes and escalate the conflict in this eventuality.

This is a case in which it is important to maintain one's side, without necessarily taking the other side, except in small ways. This is a scenario in which a transgression has occurred – when someone violates a policy, practice or human right. In this case, Adam had transgressed workplace bullying and harassment policy by causing Catherine emotional distress with his hurtful and sarcastic anger. He had been emotionally abusive, transgressing what Catherine would tolerate in her life.

Catherine said that she was raising the issue with Adam in this way because she valued her working relationship with him and it had hurt her when he had behaved in that way towards her. By saying this, she was continuing to value Adam as a person, allowing him to save face, and framing her conflict resolution efforts as something she did with people or issues she cared about. Adam finally took her side. He saw that he needed to apologise and did so. He also said he respected Catherine and didn't want their relationship to sour, nor did he want an official complaint lodged against him. He was grateful that she had spoken to him confidentially first and not gone to management or human resources. He didn't think of himself as a bully but would alter his behaviour from now on, which he did.

Their relationship was strained for the rest of the week but soon returned to normal. Adam had a new respect for Catherine and told her that he had never worked through an issue like that with anyone in a workplace environment. He never again lost his cool with Catherine.

How did Catherine feel? She felt powerful and proud! She had got what she wanted without losing it. She had taken the matter into her own hands and succeeded. She felt skilful. And she felt her relationship with Adam had grown.

If the situation had worsened or been unsuccessful, she could have then gone to her manager or human resources. As it turned out, she had protected herself, solved a conflict, saved a workplace relationship and avoided entering into an adversarial process. The point for Catherine was getting Adam to change his behaviour, not in punishing him. That was her choice.

In this scenario, it was easier for Catherine to attempt this strategy because she and Adam were equals. He did not have positional power over her – as a manager, for instance. Conflict in the workplace is a very serious and large problem, causing untold stress and tension and resulting in a hundreds of thousands of dollars being spent on grievance and discipline issues. Good communication and conflict resolution skills are essential for a vital and productive workplace.

My advice to you is to learn conflict resolution skills in order to work through minor issues with work peers. If a serious conflict develops with someone, especially if there is a positional power difference, seek advice about how to proceed.

Never suffer prolonged and unresolved conflict in your life. Always seek help. Contact a coach, counsellor, mediator or knowledgable friend or relative to help you work through the problem and take action. Chronic and unresolved conflict negatively impacts upon women's health, self-esteem, success and happiness in life. Don't let this happen to you.

Overcoming fear of conflict

Let's explore ways to overcome our fear of conflict. Most people are afraid of conflict. This is nothing to be ashamed of – it's very human. Fear is possibly the most powerful and deeply wired of all human emotions. Much of our behaviour is driven by fear. This is not necessarily a bad thing; after all, the purpose of our fear is to help us avoid danger and stay alive.

The first step to overcoming our fear of conflict is to recognise and acknowledge it. The next step is to use our fear to motivate us, not paralyse us. The exercises in this chapter look at three ways to transform our fear: by finding our voice, by viewing fear as an ally with important information for us, and by using our intuition to guide us safely through conflict. Chapter 9, Developing Clarity, also provides useful exercises on staying calm, centred and powerful during conflict.

Your voice: Being who you are in the world

Although women are still expected to take up the role of emotional caretaker, woman's role is expanding. The range of self-expression available to women is increasing all the time. For instance, in the movies women are increasingly portrayed as active heroines who do not shy from facing conflict: Meg Ryan in *Courage Under Fire*, Meryl Streep in *The River Wild*, Jodie Foster in *Silence of the Lambs* and *Contact*, Cate Blanchett in *Elizabeth*. These are women who face adversity, resolve problems and express themselves powerfully.

This new range of behaviours can best be described as 'having a voice'. 'Voice' is a social psychology term, which means having the capacity to represent yourself positively in the world, to make your presence felt in a powerful way, and to express clearly who you are and what you want. Finding our voice is a task of momentous import for women, and for all people. It is hard for men to fathom the enormity of fear many women experience when they endeavour to speak their real thoughts openly and freely, pursue their goals in the world, or ask for what they want. The old social training that it is dangerous for women to use their voice lies deep in the marrow of many women's bones.

Joy is a consultant with an impressive training background, a full practice, a teaching position and a good deal of world travel. She is bright, creative and has strong political views, yet old gender programming takes its toll on her self-esteem and sense of freedom to be herself. Joy told me recently that, irrationally, she feels inferior to many of the men in her life, though she knows this is untrue, and automatically assumes the *lesser* role in her dealings with them. Rationally, she knows better. She knows that conditioning is holding her back, yet she fears challenging men too much or taking her own side too strongly with men because 'something terrible might happen'. She feels she will be caught doing '*something illegal*'.

Taking one's own side can feel 'illegal' to many women at a deep subconscious level, though their heads tell them otherwise. They still feel undeserving. Joy said her male partner criticises her for 'not acting more powerful'. She feels shamed by these criticisms, yet cannot shake off the old belief that women are not as important as men. She, like many women today, feels sandwiched between modern expectations to be confident, independent and powerful, and the deeper, more ingrained belief in gender roles that say women should be putting their own needs second. Joy speaks for many women confronted by the complexities of today's world, in which women are expected to be more powerful and independent, yet still lack the support and tools to do so. She struggles to find her authentic female voice.

One of the questions that Joy faces is how to express herself powerfully and still honour her femininity. It is my privilege to be assisting Joy in this process, as she embarks on expanding her consulting business, developing her authentic voice in the world, and growing into her leadership.

Exercise: Finding your own voice

1. **Getting to know yourself:** One way we can cultivate our voice is by knowing our gifts, strengths and limits. Gifts are natural talents, such as being a great dancer, having an aptitude for maths or being good with animals. Strengths are character traits that you have developed over time, such as patience, kindness or courage. Limits are areas in which you have less capacity, such as being a bad cook or having trouble asking for what you want.

   This is an exercise that will help you identify your personal gifts, strengths and limits. Make three headings on a page: Gifts, Strengths and Limits. Write ten items under each heading. If you can't think of that many, ask your trusted friends for suggestions. Knowing your gifts, strengths and limits empowers you to accept credit for who you are, take responsibility for your shortcomings, set boundaries based on what works for you and what doesn't, and be able to speak clearly about who you are.

2. **Identifying life values:** Your life values give you a personal foundation from which to speak and act. Life values are what you find most fulfiling and important in life. They make life worth living. Write down the top ten things that give your life meaning, happiness and fulfilment. It could be anything: creativity, beauty, family and relationship,

nature, self-expression, justice, spirituality, humour and fun, adventure, health and healing, art, community, truth and honesty. When you have identified your values, write a short paragraph about each, what it means to you, how it fulfils you, and how you can honour that value more in your life. This values list is your personal foundation. It reflects who you are and your purpose in life. It gives you strength and authenticity.

The better you know yourself and accept yourself, the clearer your voice will be.

3. **Setting specific goals:** Developing clarity about what you want to accomplish in life can help you develop your voice. Our life goals are the manifestation of what we generally value. Otherwise they are meaningless. Based on the life values you identified, what do you really want to achieve? Write down the top five goals you want to achieve or make happen in the next five years. It is helpful to make your goals as specific as possible. For example, in the next five years you might want to buy a house, write a book, be in a committed relationship, change careers, have a baby, build a business, travel overseas. Having clear goals will help guide your actions and structure your priorities from day to day. Being clear about your goals empowers you to ask for what you want and keeps you focused. It is easier to speak up for yourself when you are clear about your goals.

Story: Ask for what you want

I once worked with a woman called Pam who was eight months'

pregnant. She wanted more companionship from her partner. On his one free day each week, he played golf with a friend. I asked her why it was difficult for her to raise this issue with him. She said, 'I'm afraid that would be selfish of me. He likes golfing.' She forced herself not to assert her need for his company rather than do or say anything that felt selfish to her. Meanwhile, her husband had no idea of her feelings, but sensed disapproval from her whenever he went golfing. This made him feel guilty and resentful, resulting in his wanting to get away from her even more. I reminded her that the new baby would not share her beliefs about being selfish and would express its needs with much gusto. How was she going to feel about that? That was a new realisation to her. I suggested that she experiment with seeing herself as a baby with lots of needs and learn to express them with relish and conviction.

Pam role played being a baby who felt entitled to have her needs met. She practised asking for more attention and affection during this time when she was pregnant and tired. 'More attention and affection right now please!' She did it in a voice that was spontaneous, winsome and direct. We both laughed. She suddenly got a sparkle in her eye and said, 'Oh, I should just *be* the baby with needs, not simply talk about it, just *show* my needs and not discuss it intellectually after the fact!' This is precisely what we need to do. We need to value our needs as lovable and acceptable, just as a baby's are.

Pam overcame her fear of selfishness and was able to ask for what she wanted in the relationship. Her husband appreciated her straightforward request and agreed to spend more time with Pam on his free days. When we accept our needs, others usually do too.

Fear as the ally

Another way to overcome our fear of conflict is to use fear as an ally. We often feel ashamed of our fear, but it is a very important emotion because it teaches us so much about ourselves and our environment. The first step is to recognise and honour our fear without judgment. It just is. There are many reasons for it. Knowing the reasons can help us understand and have compassion for ourselves. Listening to the fear provides us with important information.

For instance, fear may tell us to protect ourselves and be silent. That may be good advice in a dangerous situation, or a situation where trust has not been established. We may need first to establish trust. Or fear may caution us that the relationship is too fragile right now to bear the stress of conflict. We may need to strengthen the relationship before dealing with conflict. Fear can warn us that anger is present; if we don't want to have anger directed at us, we may need to take steps to ensure that respect and sensitivity are maintained. Fear may be telling us not to engage with this person right now. We can de-escalate peacefully. Fear can tell us that we won't be understood. We may need to build up our confidence and express our side more effectively.

Our fear tells us where our personal limits are. Sometimes we need to respect these limits. Sometimes we need to stretch beyond them and jump right over the edge. The decision is ours. The power is in knowing our fear, recognising it and making a choice to move beyond it or stay within it. Both are options that serve us at different moments. Sometimes we need to honour our fear and consciously choose not to move beyond it before we are ready.

The most reliable strategy for dealing with our fear of conflict is to become acquainted with it and to use it as a motivation to develop our communication skills. We all get scared of conflict from time to time, but knowing we have sensible and safe tools to rely on can be very reassuring. Try doing the exercise at the end of this chapter to find out what your fear is telling you.

Using our intuition

Our intuition can be immensely helpful in working through fear of conflict. Intuition is that part of us that is connected to our inner knowing, sometimes referred to us our higher self. It lets us know if we are on track in life and helps us make wise choices. It is that remarkable ability to draw the right conclusion from little or confusing information.

Our intuition can help us decide whether to go forward into a conflict, withdraw, speak up or get help. It can guide us to say the right things and help us deal with others. It is that gut-level, instinctual part of us that just 'knows' the right thing to do or say. It can also help us learn from our mistakes and assist us in understanding the deeper causes of a conflict.

People get in touch with their intuition in different ways. Some people have feelings, hunches or a sense of things. Others hear a 'voice' or see an image.

Exercise: Getting in touch with your intuition

This is a guided meditation to help you access your intuition. It is a short journey that will allow you to gain wisdom and knowledge by meeting and talking with a wise guide, a loving spirit or respected teacher – whichever image works for you.

You might want to light a candle, turn off the phone and create a safe and quiet space to do this meditation. You can have a friend read this to you, record it on a tape and play it, or simply read it as you do the exercise.

Get into a comfortable position and allow your eyes to close. Relax and let your breathing be free and easy. Continue to relax as you journey into the peace and quite of your inner world.

As you relax, let all the muscles of your body feel loose and soft, from your head down to your toes. Notice any tension areas and consciously let them go. Continue to relax, breathe easily and release your muscles. Enjoy the sensations of relaxation.

Now see a gentle veil of mist rising up before your eyes. Look at this mist carefully as it swirls before you. It is soft and white. Now watch as it slowly begins to part like two misty curtains. As it parts, you see a beautiful green lake appearing before your eyes. It is big and still and calm and surrounded by forest. It is a sacred place. See and feel the beauty and peace of this place. Let its healing energy fill your mind and body. Let the energy of this place nourish you. Enjoy this energy for a moment.

Now see a small empty rowboat pulling towards the shore you are standing on. Walk towards the boat and step inside. Sit down and be comfortable.

Now feel the boat pulling out into middle of the lake. It moves all by itself. You are journeying into the sacred world of your wise guide, spiritual teacher or helping angel.

Enjoy the ride as the boat floats gently across the lake. Feel the waves lapping softly against the side of the boat. Smell the fresh air and feel the gentle breeze touching your cheek. Relax into the slow rocking motion of the boat on the water.

As the boat draws to the far shore, you see a beautiful green forest that meets the shoreline. Get out of the boat and walk into the forest. Enjoy the fragrant and beautiful trees. Very soon you come to a door at the front of a wonderful cave made of precious stones and gems. It shines brightly. This is where your wise guide lives. She or he is inside waiting for you. Knock on the door.

Your wise guide opens the door and greets you. Notice what they look like and how they greet you. Go inside.

Inside the cave, behind the door, is the special world of your wise guide. Look around – notice the colours, the atmosphere, the essences and the surrounding features. Take it all in.

Now sit down with your wise guide. You are going to have a conversation. When you are ready, ask a question of your wise guide such as:

'Why is there so much tension between me and—?'

'What is the deeper cause of this conflict?'

'What should I do to help resolve it?'

'What should I say?'

'Is my fear real or not?'

'How should I deal with my fear?'

'What is the solution to the conflict?'

Then, sit quietly and receive the information from your wise guide. You will know when you have received the information you need because you will feel calmer, more centred and nourished from within. Thank your guide for giving you this information. Trust it and commit to following this wisdom.

Bring the conversation with your wise guide to a close. Thank them for being with you and sharing his or her wisdom.

Now stand up and leave the cave. Outside is your boat. Get into the boat. Feel your little boat moving back across the lake, to your own land. Feel the waves of the water gently rocking the boat. Now see the shore coming into view. See your house on the shore. As you step out of the boat and look back, the lake, forest, and the cave disappear behind a gentle veil of mist.

You are home again. You feel refreshed and nourished by your journey and can recall everything you want about this trip. Now gently come back into your body. Stretch and wiggle your toes. Take a breath. When you are ready, open your eyes.

Take a few minutes to recall your journey. Jot down notes about your trip.

As you gain experience at accessing your intuition, it will come more easily and quickly to you, even during a hot spat or heated conflict. You have the answers. They exist within you.

Your style in conflict

Whether we fear conflict or not, we all possess different natures and thus have different styles in dealing with conflict. Some of us see conflict as an opportunity to express ourselves and defend what we see as justice. We are Warrior Women. We may find it hard, however, to hear the other side and may try to win by the sheer force of our personality.

Others of us may seek to comfort people and keep the peace. This can have a healing effect on a situation, as we take the role of a mediator whose wise words settle people down. If this is our style, we need to guard against repressing the process of conflict and inhibiting deeper dialogue.

Or perhaps we act as an innocent bystander who has no position, preferring to be a spectator and not get involved at all. This can lead to a positive neutrality or detachment, but it can also be an abdication of responsibility.

We may react to conflict like a scared child who is terrified of pain. We feel victimised and freeze up. We want to withdraw and be safe. This sensitivity to pain can be useful if we use it to help one another understand each other's suffering and ensure that nobody is treated unfairly or cruelly. We can use our fear to act as a kind of emotional watchdog, protecting ourselves and others from being hurt.

We may approach conflict as an arbiter who tries to solve things rationally and sensibly. This can help restore a sense of safety and order. In its matter-of-factness, however, it can prevent feelings from being expressed and become overly intellectual.

Lastly, we may approach conflict as a learner who seeks understanding and connection with our conflict partner. Connection, growth and learning become the goals, rather than winning or losing.

All these styles can be useful at some time. The style we use depends on many factors including the time and place, the issue, and the personalities involved.

Regardless of our personalities or the patterns we have acquired for approaching or avoiding conflict, we will benefit from learning conflict resolution. Having skills gives us a choice about whether to play out the old habits or try something new. I am certainly no heroine when it comes to conflict.

In the past, I avoided it as much as possible. Now I avoid conflict less and know what to do when it arises. Every woman can move beyond her fear and become expert at solving inner and outer conflict and building peace in her life.

Exercise: Transforming your fear of conflict

1. Think of a conflict or tension with someone that makes you afraid.
2. Feel the fear in your body. Where is it? What does it feel like?
3. Using your imagination, visualise this feeling as an animal or creature. Give it a name if you wish (for example, a green mouse called Squeaky).
4. Imagine this animal or creature is your ally and can talk to you. It has vital information for you. Let it talk to you now. What is it afraid of? Where is the danger exactly? What unwanted thing might happen or is happening?
5. Let it now tell you what it needs *from you* to feel less afraid. What new personal quality or attitude do you need to adopt? What new positive self-belief? What step needs to be taken, if any? Do you require further help?
6. When you know what would help, let a new image arise to symbolise this new quality, attitude, belief or action. You might see an animal, creature, person or form in nature. Give it a name if you wish.
7. Hold this new image in your mind and allow it to change your posture and feeling in yourself. Notice what this is like.
8. How does this new information change your attitude or approach to the situation or conflict?

Story: Gemma's fear – mouse and dinosaur

This story might help you to put the above exercise into practice. I once had a colleague who was wonderful but somewhat intimidating, so I did the exercise. My fear was mostly located in my chest, which I visualised as a little mouse called Squeaky. Squeaky was afraid of my colleague's somewhat confrontational and superior style. It made Squeaky feel inferior and intimidated. Squeaky wanted me to feel more confident around this person, to believe that I was equal to her, and to act bigger around her. The new image that arose to symbolise this confidence, belief in my equality, and acting-bigger behaviour was a red plastic blow-up dinosaur called Rex. I really needed to puff myself up around this colleague! Next time I spoke with her, I let Rex do the talking. Instead of acting smaller or discussing work difficulties, I shared how well I was doing and all the great things that were happening for me. What a difference it made! My goal became to equalise our relationship and stop underselling myself. I felt better about my colleague too.

Thoughts to hold
- Fear is a natural, ancient, flight-or-fight response to a perceived threat such as conflict.
- Women can suffer additional fear of conflict due to social conditioning and our desire to preserve harmonious relationships.
- Without positive models for resolving conflict, we fear and avoid it.

- Fear can become an ally when we listen to and learn from it.
- It is your right as a human being to have your own viewpoint and to express it without fear of harm, domination or ridicule.
- Your intuition can assist you in overcoming fear of conflict and choosing the right path of action for you.

9 Developing Clarity

It seems to me that . . . women have been developing their masculine qualities: getting out and exploring and exercising their talents in the world and fighting for equality and obtaining their rights. This is admirable and fine. Nevertheless what is needed now is the development of their feminine strength and the feminine strength of men.

Scilla Elworthy

Being clear and centred is the biggest help of all in conflict. But it is often the last thing we feel. When tension is present, we usually feel out of sorts, afraid, defensive and worried. This is human. So how can we find clarity and remain centred and aware? How can we be our best selves and care for both our own needs and the needs of others? How can we trust the process and show up with an open heart, despite the many aggravations of conflict? This chapter explores some of the ways we lose our centre during conflict and offers ideas on how to stay clear-headed.

Women losing their centre

During my conflict resolution classes for women, I noticed a curious thing – the mere mention of conflict sent some women into outer orbit. They spaced out and were unable to think or speak clearly. They lost their ground and felt confused about how to proceed or what to say. They found it difficult to take their own side or to be clear about what they wanted and needed in a conflict. They failed to comprehend what the other side was saying to them.

In the following section we look at key issues that undermine a woman's ability to be calm and confident in a conflict.

Barriers to clarity

Dependency

Actual or perceived dependency on another can often compromise a woman's sense of safety and freedom to discuss issues. This dynamic is a potential problem in any relationship where power is unequal, whether between boss and employee, teacher and student or adult and child, as well as in partnerships where one is supporting the other financially. The more dependent we perceive ourselves to be, the more we may hesitate to oppose the other side. We may feel the need to please if we think our security is dependent on their goodwill. Of course, in a healthy relationship, both people should feel safe to speak up, regardless of differences in power.

Even if in our current conflict we are in fact safe to express ourselves, our past conditioning can create the same barrier. These unspoken issues of fear, power and insecurity are often operating unconsciously when we are in conflict and can alter our mental state to a point where we lose our centre, our sense of self. We may have so much inner conflict going on that we can hardly focus on the outer discussion or act effectively. We revert to old coping strategies such as appeasement, silence, anger or manipulation. We are pretending to listen but are not really present, not centred, not in a place of authenticity, of personal power. We appear to be present but, in actual fact, are emotionally absent. We have 'left'.

Sudden shock factor

Another reason we become unbalanced and ungrounded during conflict is because we aren't prepared for it. Its sudden appearance shocks us. All military strategists understand the psychological impact of surprise. It shocks, disorientates and momentarily paralyses. If someone initiates a conflict with us, we can minimise the shock factor by asking for some time to prepare before talking about it. Similarly, we can prepare the other person before springing a conflict on them suddenly. I don't recommend just sliding into conflict unconsciously. It works better and shows respect if we ask permission to discuss an issue first. If necessary, we can set up a time and place to talk that feels safe for both sides. In an ongoing relationship, it may be helpful to establish a regular time and place for conflicts or differences to help eliminate the shock factor.

Getting hurt and the zap factor

We can also lose our centre during conflict when someone says something that is hurtful to us. Instead of dealing with it directly we often will become disconnected from our feelings. Half an hour or a week later we come to our senses and think, 'OUCH! That hurt!'

Why are our reactions delayed? Why do we lose our centre when something hurtful is said? One of the main reasons is shock and lack of preparedness, as discussed above.

Another reason for a delayed reaction is an instinctual protective response designed to prevent us from doing or saying anything that might make matters worse. Something in us freezes until the danger passes.

We may also have a delayed reaction when we are hurt if the current situation reminds us of an old wound. We may find ourselves suddenly conscious of old memories and pains. This may go on at an unconscious level, in effect shutting us off from what is going on in the present time.

If we find ourselves paralysed in a conflict, it is usually because we are feeling hurt, frightened, angry or shocked but are unable to communicate it. These reactions become split off. This splitting happens when we reach a limit or a block in our communication. We hit a wall and cannot respond. We are unable to voice our feelings because of belief systems which tells us we should not be hurt or angry in the first place, or that we should not spoil things by saying so. We feel embarrassed for feeling hurt. We fear that if we express our feelings directly, we may be called difficult, overly sensitive or controlling. Sometimes, just saying that we feel hurt creates an opportunity to come back to the present. We can then say what we need in order to feel better, whether a few moments to collect ourselves, reassurance from the other side, a third party to mediate, agreed-upon ground-rules, encouragement to take our own side, a postponement of the matter until a later time or an apology.

Lack of time

To resolve tensions we need to get together and talk openly and honestly. I often ask couples in conflict, 'Have you talked about this together?' and more often than not, the answer is 'No'. Finding the time to do this is often difficult in today's world of dual careers and speedy living. But people tend to get more frustrated or more confused about their feelings the longer they wait. If peace in our relationships is a high priority, we need to make the time in our busy schedule for conflict resolution.

We should agree to a time and a place when we can sit together in peace. An hour is preferable to go to the depths of an issue, but we may need a series of shorter meetings before resolution occurs. It is rarely productive to meet late at night or when one or both people are tired. Some couples set aside time once a week to work on an issue that may take many months to resolve. Things take time but only if we take the time. It is important to acknowledge ourselves for taking the necessary time and not to get discouraged if a conflict doesn't resolve overnight. In very heated conflicts we may need to time the session and when the time is up, stop, unless both sides agree to go further. This creates manageable and digestible pieces of work that build confidence and reduce fear.

Need to please

Needing to please means that our focus is on gaining approval from the other side and not in resolving the issue at hand. Trying to please others gets us lost as we become increasingly confused between our side and theirs. It throws us off centre quicker than anything else. To regain our centre and sense of perspective, we need to remind ourselves that we are lovable when we are being true to our selves. We need to please our own heart first.

Emotion

Getting into an emotional state is the main reason we lose our centre during conflict. If we are angry, hurt, scared, frustrated or sad, it is hard to focus clearly on the issue. We lose our objectivity and ability to remain calm and clear. Conflict is an emotional process, so staying centred and clear can be a challenge. However, it is possible to regain our centre in the midst of emotion. The following section offers ideas for how to remain calm and clear during conflict.

How to overcome barriers to clarity

Inner preparation

Having decided to focus on an issue, you may want to do some inner work to help you prepare. Preparation is a great way to stay centred and grounded. Here are some questions you can ask yourself ahead of time to help you prepare:

- What am I unhappy about?
- What do I want to get out of this conversation?
- How can we use this problem to strengthen our relationship?
- Am I taking my stress out on this person?
- Am I avoiding my own problems?
- What is the real issue we need to look at?
- Is this conflict really between me and this person, or between me and someone else?

Creating trust and safety

When you finally meet to talk, you can both become grounded and centred by honouring and thanking each other for being willing to come together to find resolution. You can both agree to strive for honesty and complete resolution. This helps create a container of mutual respect and positive intention for the work that follows. Here are some sample statements of things you might say to begin the process:

- Thank you for coming. I am grateful.
- I want to hear and understand you.
- I will do my best to be honest and truthful.
- I honour us both for doing this work.
- Everything that is said here is confidential
- I want the best outcome for both of us.
- Co-operation is more important than winning.
- I believe we can work this out together.

Staying grounded in the process

Once you are engaged in the conflict, take a moment to focus on yourself. Become aware of your thoughts and feelings about the issue in question. You may feel ready to take your own side or you may want to apologise or take the other side. You may feel removed from the conflict and just want to see what happens. If you feel closer to the other side or neutral, let the other person begin first.

You can establish your centre at any time by asking yourself these three simple questions: *Where am I in the moment? What am I feeling? Which side am I on now?*

1. **Am I on my side?** Do you feel tense or upset? If so, take your side. Express your feelings, thoughts, needs and opinions on the matter and then check yourself again. Try to speak from the heart and guts. It saves time and pain.

Forget the intellectualisations. Get to the point of how you feel. Be brave.

2. **Am I on the other side?** Do you feel open, interested, concerned about or understanding of the other person? Do you agree with them, even in part? If so, take their side by showing your understanding. Say it with feeling. Don't be aloof. Show that you *really* get it.

3. **Am I neutral?** Do you feel detached or disengaged from the conflict? If so, stand back and look at the overall situation. Offer suggestions as to what you or your conflict partner might do to remedy the situation. Make sure you are truly neutral, calm and fair, and not remote or disconnected.

Use body awareness techniques

Another useful tool to help you stay grounded and centred is to use body awareness techniques. Make sure you are physically comfortable. Put your feet on the floor so that the energy of the earth can support and nourish you. Lengthen your spine so that you are sitting up straight and can breathe fully and naturally. If you get scared or upset, remember to keep breathing. Keep your head up and make eye contact with the person.

By aligning your body with the earth and lifting your upper torso and head, you create the appearance of strength and clarity. You will also *feel* stronger, clearer and more grounded. You do not have to do this in an exaggerated way and become stiff and formal. Do it in a soft and gentle way, holding yourself present and alert and allowing the natural energy of your body to support and hold you. When you feel yourself beginning to crumple, gently bring yourself back to this strengthening align-ment and breathe easily. Silently ask the earth to support and ground you.

If you get really tense, you can also place your hand on your lower abdomen to centre and hold you. Imagine that your lower abdomen is a container of love, security, power and warmth. Feel its nourishing and grounding energy. Know that whatever happens in the conflict, you can deal with it.

There are many books available today on how to centre your energy. Use any of your favourite meditation, yoga or breathing techniques to minimise anxiety and create stability within.

The following stories are about two women who learned to find their centre in a conflict.

Story 1: Self-defence – the porcupine

Celeste is a young woman in a new relationship. She feels weak in relation to her partner who, according to her, dominates her. She says she falls into a trance she describes as 'passive aggres-sive'. When her partner doesn't help with a household task she requests of him, she becomes irritated and snips sarcastically, 'Fine! Don't then! Don't help at all. That's just FINE!' Of course, it isn't fine but Celeste doesn't know how else to take her own side. I asked her to exaggerate this state of passive aggression for the purposes of exploration. She said she experienced this state as happening outside of her control. We often feel out of control of our behaviour during conflict, but by duplicating the same state slowly at a later time we can learn a lot about ourselves.

I asked Celeste to make her reactions big and dramatic. She flung her arms wide and yelled, 'THAT'S JUST FINE!' As she did this, she used pushing away motions with her hands and contracted her body as if she was keeping out an unwanted force. She said she felt defensive. I suggested that she defend herself more directly, without the sarcasm. She said she felt like a porcupine, all rolled up with its quills out. I told her to go ahead and be as self-protective as a porcupine, that she must need the defence system of a porcupine for some reason. This was hard for her. It felt wrong to her to be so defensive. I suggested that her defensiveness had been happening indirectly and perhaps destructively, so why not learn to do it consciously? Expressed passively, her defence was ineffective. Celeste complained that her porcupine quills went everywhere and never met their mark. She couldn't shoot straight with even one quill. The energy of the porcupine was potentially quite wonderful but not yet aimed right. Her energy was scattered and not at all centred.

I offered to model being a porcupine that aimed straight with its quills. Celeste role played her conflict partner, John. Playing him, she said, 'Just get real!' in a superior tone of voice. I said, as porcupine–Celeste, 'Don't talk to me like that. It's a put-down.' He said, 'That's reality! Get used to it!' I said, 'How you are putting me down hurts and angers me. I want you to listen to my reality.' Suddenly Celeste stopped the role-play and said, 'Oh no, if I said that, he'd feel badly, as if he were abusing his power'. 'Well, maybe he is somewhat,' I answered. She looked at me wide-eyed. Though it seemed obvious to me, the idea had never occurred to her that her defensiveness might be related to his put-downs. To be fair, his frustration with her was probably related to her lack of direct communication. Both of them communicated poorly with their sarcasm and said very little with it! Celeste went back home and was direct with her feelings. She said what she felt, rather than being sarcastic. Her quill hit its target. Real communication began to happen between John and Celeste. As Celeste learned to find her centre and stay calm, John began communicating more directly as well. They found themselves understanding each other more deeply.

Story 2: Self-protection – the wall of ice

Therese noticed that she often went into a frozen state whenever she and her husband fought. His rationality and forceful style always made her feel stupid and tongue-tied, like a naughty child who had done something wrong. Her speech would become fragmented and erratic and her eyes would glaze over as she lamely attempted to defend herself. A wall of ice encased her heart and mind, making it impossible for her to be centred, or even speak coherently. Her husband would grow increasingly irritated by her broken communication.

Through working on herself, Therese became increasingly aware of this frozen state that occurred during arguments with her husband. She became aware of how this frozen state reminded her of her childhood and of her father who always yelled at her and called her 'stupid'. She withdrew behind the wall of ice.

I asked her to explore the wall of ice. Therese said it was a wall of protection, a way of detaching from what was happening. Therese needed this icy detachment to stand up to her husband's forceful style. I encouraged her to speak like an icy wall. Therese tried it. She said, 'Stop. I don't like your tone of voice. You're berating me'. Sharp, clear, and to the point. As Therese learned to trust her instinctual response of freezing up in the face of force and criticism she began to claim her own voice and demanded to be heard. Unfortunately, her husband was unable to meet these new demands for respect and continued to berate Therese. After much consideration and couples therapy, they decided to part ways. But Therese had learned a powerful lesson about finding her voice and standing her ground and went on to find a wonderful man more in keeping with who she was now, a clear-headed and self-respecting woman.

Gemma's clarity preparation

This is what I do to prepare myself for a conflict to ensure that I maintain my centre and stay clear-headed.

1. First, I try to make a time to talk with the person concerned. If I can't do that, I say that I am aware that the other person and I have a conflict and that we need to discuss the issue together. This gives us both a chance to steady ourselves and be mindful. Conflict resolution is the art of mindfulness – knowing what you are doing in any given moment.

2. If I have time to prepare beforehand, I sit and meditate on the conflict. I write down my thoughts, feelings and reactions. I allow myself to express feelings of self-pity, fear or anger. Then after I've cooled down, I see what issues still feel important to discuss. This is knowing my bottom-line – what must be said or addressed and what I want.

3. I imagine having the debate and go through various scenarios in my head. As I go through this imaginative dialogue, I listen carefully for things I say that sound particularly truthful or direct. There are certain things we say that ring with clarity and substance. These are usually the 'I-statements' that reveal our side, what our experience is, and what we want. In this practice session, I am essentially getting to know my own thoughts and feelings on the matter and getting to the core of my side. This will be the essential message I want to convey.

4. I also try to imagine how the other side might feel and respond to me. I imagine what they might say, not so I can cook up arguments against it, but so that I can begin to reflect on another point of view. There is always another side, and I never expect someone just to lie down and accept what I have to say. I expect to hear a different perspective from my own.

5. If the other person has initiated the conflict, I try to see where their complaint or accusation is true. I check inside myself to see if I think their accusation is a fair one. Then when I meet with them I don't have to waste time defending myself, if what is required is an explanation or apology.

6. Finally, I ask myself what I hope to achieve from this conflict. What change would I like to see happen? What do I need from the other side? What would resolution look like for me? If I am afraid of the meeting and fear that I won't be able to take my side, I call a support person to help me prepare.

Exercise: Knowing your emotions in conflict

Many of us avoid conflict because we feel uncomfortable with the emotions and feelings that come up such as fear, anger, guilt and helplessness. We feel 'taken over' by these emotions and become blocked, frozen and unable to react. The following exercise will help you become more aware of your emotional states during conflict.

1. Recall a strong emotion or feeling that you experienced during a conflict. For example, you may have felt fearful and unable to say much, or you may have felt hurt and become silent and withdrawn, or you may have become angry and were unable to cool down.

2. Describe it fully: what did it feel like, how did you look and sound?

3. Dramatise the feelings. If you were trembling with fear, really shake. If you felt anger, stomp and yell. If you felt like running, let yourself run around the room. If you felt stunned or shocked, stare into space. Dramatise your emotional state so that you can study it in detail.

4. What is the message of this feeling? Articulate it in one sentence: 'My feelings tell me that I . . .'

5. What did you learn about yourself from examining your feelings? Imagine how you might apply this information to the conflict. What would you say now that you couldn't before?

6. What techniques help you stay centred and calm in general? Posture, breathing, self-awareness, being prepared, having ground rules? How can you use these techniques to manage your emotions better in the future?

Thoughts to hold

- We often lose our centre in conflict when we experience strong emotions.
- Preparing ourselves ahead of time helps us stay grounded and clear in conflict.
- When we lose our centre we can stop, check our feelings, and communicate them.
- Believing that it is okay to take our side can helps us stay centred.
- Knowing what we want gives us clarity and confidence.

10 Inner Conflict: Trouble Within

Nothing in life is to be feared, it is only to be understood.

Marie Curie

Inner conflict looks very much like outer conflict, only it is happening inside us. I have inner conflicts often. Usually they are small ones, but sometimes they are big. I also have inner conflicts that are part of my long-term development as an individual. These long-term issues provide material for personal growth work. Some of these long-term conflicts have to do with my feelings of self-worth, or with my sense of freedom to follow my creativity, or my belief in love. We are all on the path of personal development in our own unique way. Working with our inner conflicts can speed up the process of change and increase our self-knowledge and inner peace.

Inner conflict is normal, cyclic, and an intrinsic part of how we grow. Some conflicts are small and inconsequential, such as whether to wash the dishes after dinner or tomorrow morning. Some are complex or difficult and need the help of a support person in the form of a therapist, life coach, trusted friend, partner or support group. Some inner conflicts may even stem from deep childhood wounds or other oppressive circumstances.

What inner conflicts do you have? Perhaps you struggle over whether you are truly lovable or good enough, or whether it is okay to get angry or to want time alone. Maybe you struggle over whether you can ever be the artist or creative woman you dreamed of being as a young girl, or whether you can survive in the world on your own, pay the bills and raise the children. You might have ambivalent feelings toward your significant other, or feel torn between your need to be looked after and your longing to become your own person and follow your independent dream. You may struggle to find meaning in life and to understand the fears that hold you back. You may feel torn about helping the world and pursuing your own happiness.

Inner conflicts that are avoided for long periods of time can lead to body symptoms or to feelings of depression or anxiety. Inner conflict can give us headaches, stomach cramps, sour moods, or sleepless nights. We often experience inner conflict as an argument in our head that can make us feel torn, confused and troubled. We think we should be different from the way we are. We don't know if we should do one thing or another, we have competing feelings or opinions. Often the discomfort of these symptoms become the impetus for us to look at issues we are avoiding in our lives.

Finding inner balance

Inner conflict looks very much like outer conflict, except instead of two people we have two parts of ourselves in conflict. When we work on an inner conflict, we need to identify these two parts, This Side and The Other Side. But there will also be the Neutral Side, that wise part of us that witnesses the conflict and helps to resolve it with love and patience. It is very helpful to cultivate the Fair Witness within.

One woman described inner conflict not as two competing sides in her head but a whole committee of conflicting opinions! Often we do have the sense of carrying our whole family or society in our heads, all yelling and screaming about what kind of woman we should be. But inner conflict usually breaks down into two main sides or points of view, just as outer conflict does. As we work on our inner conflicts, we may notice that one side is louder and more dominant than the other, or that one side is always telling the other what to do. There are power struggles inside our heads. Inner conflict resolution helps us find balance and peace within.

Growing into wisdom

Inner conflict occurs regularly. The wheels of the psyche spark against each other, creating the motivation and energy for change and the development of our minds, bodies and souls. Inner conflict provides us with sufficient dilemmas in life to motivate us to reach up and access our higher selves, that part of us that is interested growing and not merely surviving.

Working through our inner conflicts can make us strong and wise, and teach us how to connect with other humans as part of our own vulnerable humanity. Through inner struggle, we develop our compassion and love for ourselves and others. Every wise woman has wrestled with her own inner demons and found self-acceptance and peace. Exploring our inner dilemmas can illuminate the doorway through which we discover our purpose in life and find meaning for ourselves.

Working on our inner conflicts is good for:

- resolving unfinished business from the past
- resolving tensions with others when we cannot do it with the actual person
- forgiving conflicts with others that need to be forgiven
- helping us get unstuck in our lives
- helping us make decisions and choices in our lives
- working through our fears and blocks
- developing our authenticity, power and strength
- connecting us with our creativity, intuition and inner knowledge
- developing self-awareness, strength and resilience

How to work on inner conflict

Working on our inner conflicts uses the same three steps we use for outer conflicts, with some modifications. Let's look at an example.

I have a conflict within myself about whether to laze around all day Saturday or work on my projects, do my housework, and generally be 'productive'. I want to relax and do nothing after a week of work, but also feel that I should do things like cleaning, shopping and reading professional articles. The 'Worker' in me thinks that the 'Lazy One' is a couch potato. The 'Lazy One' thinks the 'Worker' is a taskmaster.

When I listen carefully to my inner dialogue, I notice that the 'Worker' sounds self-assured, smug and almost parental. I know the 'Worker' side very well. I think of myself as a good, solid worker. The 'Lazy One' sounds insecure and a little guilty. I know this side less well.

Very often with inner conflict (as with outer conflict) one side is more dominant and has an easier time taking their side. The other side, in contrast, is usually less steady, unsure of themselves and has trouble taking their own side. It needs a little extra encouragement to do so. This may be a newer aspect of ourselves attempting to emerge and express itself, or a part of us that has remained buried or voiceless since childhood.

I continue to listen to the dialogue between my 'Worker' and 'Lazy One'. I become aware that I tend to be critical toward that part of myself that wants to lie down and do nothing. The fact that I call it a derogatory name, the 'Lazy One', shows me how much I disapprove of it. Seeing this, from the neutral position, I decide to let the 'Lazy One' talk. I ask it what it really wants and support it to take its side.

The 'Lazy One' says that it wants a different experience from the usual routine. It wants some down time. It needs a break. I listen some more. The 'Lazy One' doesn't want just any break. It wants to feel refreshed, revitalised, renewed. It wants a sense of spiritual revival. It feels burned out! Behind the 'Lazy One's desire for rest is a deep need to experience silence, serenity, something that nourishes the soul and spirit.

Often we don't know what we really need until we listen to the less dominant inner voice, believe in it and give it time to discover its message. Listening and asking questions is important, just as it is with another person. This encounter between the 'Worker' and the 'Lazy One' was a true conflict of mine and it was from this exploration that I decided to take a month off work and go live on the coast to write the first draft of this book. What a risk I felt I was taking: how could I afford it? I didn't know how to write a book!

Nourishing and supporting my creativity is one of my highest goals in life, yet it can be hard to serve this goal amid the noise and pace of everyday life. Too often, it gets put on hold. I have discovered that space, silence and time on my own are often required for my creative juices to flow. Doing nothing and being quiet is often the doorway to my creative self-expression. Being creative renews my spirit.

The address of the little cottage I rented beside the ocean was Gender Drive! Another amazing thing about this month was that when I told my clients what I was doing, they positively cheered! Even my beautician got inspired and said she was going to spend a week at the beach to design and sew clothes, her secret creative wish. The support was overwhelming. That is the power of facing your inner conflicts.

Skills required to work on our inner conflicts
- Self-love and compassion
- Patience and interest
- Ability to really listen to the voices within
- Belief in ourselves that we can solve our problems
- Courage to be completely honest with ourselves

The links between inner and outer conflict

We all know that somehow our outer and inner worlds are linked. Working through an inner conflict often allows us to make wise choices that reduce the outer conflict in our life. For instance, when we work on our inner critic and stop listening to that destructive voice in our head, we often choose not to associate with critical or negative people in our outer lives. We also become less critical of others.

Likewise, working on our outer problems with people can resolve our inner conflicts. For instance, when we deal effectively with an outer difficulty with someone, it raises our self-esteem, clarifies our mind and builds our inner strength.

Story 1: Depression and the critic – Ruby's dilemma

Ruby was diagnosed with depression. As a child she had wanted to become a doctor but was told by her family she wasn't smart enough. This was based on nothing other than the fact that she was a girl. Sadly, she internalised the message that she was stupid. So she became a secretary instead of a doctor. Over the years, Ruby became very overweight and very depressed. She had a recurring dream of going up a long flight of stairs and then falling down when she got to the top. Something always toppled her whenever she reached the top stair.

Ruby had an Inner Toppler that would never let her reach for her goals in life. Interestingly, she wore massive ornate earrings and drove a fiery red sports car. Ruby had tons of style, energy and ambition that had never been supported or realised.

I worked with Ruby to help her believe in herself and to become aware of her inner conflict over whether or not she was smart enough to reach her goals in life. She was obviously a very intelligent woman who could have achieved her goals.

Ruby's conflict is very common and involves an 'inner critic'. The inner critic is often formed early in life and comes from internalising the negative messages we received about ourselves from parents, school and society. It is often perfectionistic and demanding. Like Ruby, many of us feel depressed and beat ourselves up for agreeing with the low expectations others hold for us, or for not meeting parental or social expectations of how we should be. Many women are plagued with doubts and self-criticisms about not being the 'right' kind of woman, not being pretty, smart or good enough. This is not surprising given the deluge of societal and media messages portraying women in submissive or secondary roles, while at the same time exhorting them to be thinner, more beautiful and more successful in home and work life.

This kind of inner beating up often goes unnoticed at the conscious level because it is so habitual. It is the background Muzak of our minds. But by noticing these inner tensions and working on them we can become aware of the ways we hold ourselves back or push ourselves to be perfect, and in the process deny our deeper purpose in life.

Ruby worked hard to overcome her inner critic and embrace her self-worth and intelligence. She joined a Toastmasters club as a way to gain confidence in herself. Next, she saw a nutritional consultant to help her eat better and reduce weight. Ruby said she was now 'feeding her dreams, not her demons'. Finally, Ruby went back to finish her high school diploma. She was determined to become a nurse, possibly a nurse educator.

It is never too late to embark on our dreams. Recently in a workshop I gave on 'following your dreams', a seventy-year-old woman stood up in the group and announced that she was going back to school! She had always regretted not having more education in her life but now wanted to embrace this dream.

In the next inner conflict, we look at one woman's dilemma over her outer physical appearance and her inner spiritual life. This inner conflict is also a common dilemma for women who feel valued only for their physical beauty.

Story 2: The inner and outer woman – Monica's hair

Monica was a twenty-five-year-old make-up artist who felt concerned about the fact she no longer wanted to wash her hair every day. For Monica, washing her hair meant shampooing, conditioning, drying, setting and spraying to achieve the perfect look she felt she needed to face the world each day. But this took so much time she didn't have time left to meditate, read the newspaper or relax before going to work. As a woman who simply gives her hair a quick brush in the morning, I was intrigued and a little puzzled by this dilemma.

Monica was a scrupulously clean and organised woman with never a hair out of place. But something new inside her was pushing its way into her life. The conflict over hair was symptomatic of a deeper conflict to do with Monica's emerging spiritual life. Monica had always run a tight ship in her house, as well as with her appearance, but as she got older she wanted to let go of this compulsion and to feel good about being 'imperfect'. She wanted more time for her inner life, especially in the mornings, but was anxious about letting go of her hair routine. Her desire to have more time for self-reflection and personal leisure conflicted with her need to look polished for work and the world outside. To resolve this conflict she needed to set aside the 'outer woman' and begin listening to the 'inner woman'. The 'inner woman', the part of Monica that wanted time to focus on internal needs, spoke in a small, insecure voice. That little voice needed support and validation.

Monica had received lots of positive reinforcement in her life for looking great on the outside, as many women do. She was considered a very pretty little girl with beautiful blonde hair. She had also been sexually abused as a child and as a result, often felt as if she needed to keep herself under control. Giving up that control presented a conflict for Monica because keeping up her appearance and keeping her house clean made her feel safe. Would spending time in quite reflection also be safe or would it threaten her sense of security?

I asked Monica to take both sides of the conflict, the perfectionist 'Outer Woman' and the messy 'Inner Woman', who desired time for other things. Gradually, with coaching, she was able to stand up for the 'messy one' and support her need to take time for her inner life. After working on the conflict, Monica decided she wanted to relax her appearance and just enjoy being herself. She went out and bought a baseball cap and just plonked it on her head! That was the end of the hair treatments. I thought she looked smashing. Her hair looked fine, even without the long beauty treatment every morning. Fortunately, Monica's career in fashion allowed her to make this radical departure in style without raising eyebrows. But even if she had worked in a formal corporate setting, she could have easily created a hairstyle that didn't require excessive maintenance.

This was a true *inner* conflict, not one that others would have noticed. Now Monica saves herself 60 minutes of free time each morning. Enough time to have a whole other life. She now spends each morning meditating, writing in her journal and reading the newspaper. Our inner life can often get neglected in the quest to be the 'beautiful woman' for others in our appearance and behaviour.

What we avoid or deny in ourselves may haunt us through body symptoms, relationship problems or nagging internal self-criticisms. But as we see in the examples above, these disturbances, however trying, also carry messages for our growth. Our inner conflicts provide vital opportunities to learn about important parts of ourselves. As we work with the conflict we gain new insights about ourselves, which lead to new choices about how to proceed in life.

The next story is about a conflict that is increasingly found in today's workaholic world.

Story 3: Serving the world and serving the self – Annie's case of fire and water

Annie was a social activist working long and irregular hours for a community organisation. She often felt overburdened by the pressure of work and found herself awake at night, unable to sleep because her mind was continually racing, trying to figure out solutions to problems at work. One part of her was so tired that she would have done anything to get some rest, but the working part of her was on fire all the time. She often had colds and flus because she was tired to the point of being run down. But she couldn't stop. They needed her and there was so much to do.

One night she dreamed of hurtling down a hillside in her car, out of control. Another night she dreamed of being chased by a man with a big red head. This big red head reminded her of her own buzzing head full of aches and pains. But she just couldn't let go of her struggles and any attempts to get her to work less made her feel unsupported. Activism was her life. It was her passion, her fire.

Annie had a genuine conflict between her activism and her need for quiet introversion and rest. When we explored the fiery side of her, full of pressure and energy, she told moving stories of the importance of her work but also how alone and unsupported she felt in it. She complained of a co-worker who was constantly panicked and needing Annie to calm her down. At home, Annie's boyfriend pulled on her time and attention. Though generally supportive, he resented the amount of energy Annie's job consumed. Annie felt as if she was always giving. She knew she was overly responsible yet she couldn't stop.

While working on her stress, she recalled a memory from childhood in which she threw a homework assignment in the garbage because she felt it wasn't 'good enough'. Annie remembered school as a stressful time of always trying to do better. In her family of origin, she was the eldest, the stable one, the one who was there to help everyone else.

The tired side of her just wanted to rest. She flip-flopped between these two parts of herself, between over-working and exhaustion. But the fiery 'activist' side of her also needed support. This side of Annie was not willing to rest until some of the problems at work had been solved. Resting was her deeper need but she couldn't satisfy this need without negotiating a deal with her hot-headed self. The deal she finally negotiated with herself was to make more boundaries at home and work.

She set a boundary with her co-worker and told her she wasn't available to help her with her feelings and did not want to be interrupted. At home, she made it clear to her boyfriend she needed space and time to recover from work before they started doing things together as a couple in the evenings. She asked her boyfriend to give her thirty minutes after work to finish up loose ends from work, complete phone calls and unwind. She also realised she needed to get support for her highly stressful job. She arranged to talk to a friend in the same field about her stress and started cultivating other forms of professional support.

Annie needed to cool down and look after herself. The first step was to create boundaries and support systems that would act to contain the fire. Annie did finally resign from her job and created a new life for herself, based more on her own internal needs and less on social activism. She realised, however, that her need to serve others was genuine but that she wanted to do it in a way that was more balanced and nourishing for her. She knew that in the future she would need to maintain a balance between her need for self-focus and her need to be of service to others.

Annie had an inner conflict between two sides of herself: the 'Political Activist' and the 'Spiritual Hermit'. In today's busy world, many women face a similar dilemma. We try to succeed at all levels of life: work, family, friends and civic service. We try to give as much of ourselves as we can while still reserving some energy for our inner lives. Occasionally I see a woman with repressed ambitions who is underachieving in her life and who needs a push to overcome her fears and face the world. But more often I see stressed-out women who desperately need a quiet space for themselves to think, read, write, muse, reflect, dream and relax. We all need a place where we do not have to give anything to anyone but ourselves.

In the next conflict we see a woman whose body told her which direction she needed to go.

Story 4: Self-neglect and self-care – Pauline's bronchitis

Pauline was a divorced woman in her thirties who worked as a programmer for a software company. One morning she found herself sick with bronchitis. She said she was distressed about missing work. I could hear her laboured breathing and knew she was quite ill, but she couldn't accept this for some reason. She told me of an inner voice that said she was weak and making it up. I asked where this voice came from and she told me her mother was a doctor who tolerated no 'weakness'.

As a child, Pauline once had a sore arm and went to her mother for help. Her mother placed a bandage on Pauline's arm, very tight. Pauline's arm quickly began to swell and ache under the tight bandage, so she returned to her mother to take off the bandage. Her mother said, 'That'll teach you'. The lesson she drew from this was that pain and illness is a weakness that will not be tolerated.

Pauline needed to become aware of the restricting beliefs she had internalised from her mother. The first belief was that she was 'faking it' whenever she felt sick, tired, or unable to go on. The 'Inner Doctor' in her was a harsh one that belittled her pain. This made her vulnerable to overworking herself and not respecting her energy limits. It also made her unable to reject other people's excessive demands upon her time and energy. Her inability to stand up for herself and set firm boundaries created a debilitating passivity in Pauline. She couldn't say no to others. This kind of self-martyrdom is common in women who have been encouraged to dismiss their own needs and see their role as servers of others' needs.

Pauline needed to support the 'Weak One' within herself. Her illness asked her to get in touch with her needs and to stop viewing herself as an endless giver of energy. After working on this conflict Pauline went home and promptly took off two weeks from work. Interestingly, after this bout of illness, she started becoming more assertive. Perhaps it was the simple act of taking her own physical needs seriously that prompted the emotional shift. Perhaps it was just having the time to nourish her deeper needs. Pauline decided she wanted to work on the reasons she overextended herself. She started saying 'No' to more people and began to examine the ways she allowed others to tell her what to do and how to live her life. She began to look after herself and stay in touch with her own needs.

Pauline's bronchitis taught her two things: how to say 'No' to outer pressures that drained her, and how to develop a more nurturing and less harsh attitude toward her own needs and limits. As her story illustrates, body symptoms are a common way in which inner conflicts get expressed. When we are too one-sidedly ambitious, work-oriented or selfless, we get tired and run-down; this makes us more vulnerable to stress related illness. Of course, genetics, diet and environment all conspire to predispose us to certain types of symptoms. However, failing to deal with inner tensions creates additional stress on the body.

Resolving it within: A small town in my head

Often we feel tensions with someone in our current life but are not in a position to address it with them. Then resolving it internally can be helpful. While I was writing this book I met Sarah, a delightful writer. We met for lunch and excitedly shared our ideas. I told her about my book on conflict and she promptly told me what it was like living in a small rural town where she ran into people all the time, including those people she didn't like or had unfinished business with. She told me about one woman she just couldn't get along with, yet it didn't feel right to discuss the matter with her. My writer friend was also a therapist and feared that if she attempted to resolve the issue with this woman and it didn't succeed, the woman would gossip about her and tarnish her professional reputation. She thought it best to let sleeping dogs lie. I could sympathise with the unique relationship problems of a small town.

Sarah was clear about not wanting to resolve the tension externally with the woman, so I suggested she try to resolve it internally. She liked this idea. She felt she needed to find inner peace in the matter in order to feel secure about bumping into her 'foe' at the supermarket.

The following is the exercise I gave Sarah. It can be used to gain insight and resolution in many conflicts.

Think of a person that makes you feel uncomfortable or upset. It may be a situation where you feel disliked or perhaps you are irritated and are avoiding the person. Picture the person and recall the details of a particularly bad moment between you: what they looked like, what they said, how you felt, who else was there. Now, in your imagination, say all the things you didn't say at the time. Have all your reactions. Remember, this is about clearing yourself and unclogging your emotional arteries. Say everything on your mind; don't stop until you feel complete. Express your side fully. Be entirely one-sided. Even be a little self-righteous if necessary.

Now check and see how you feel. How does the other person look now? In your imagination, let them respond. Let them say everything you imagine they would say. Let them take their own side. Listen carefully to their viewpoint. Ask them questions and have them answer. Now take your side again. Stick to your gut feelings. Let them do likewise. Go back and forth until both of you are done, spent or understand each other better.

Check the emotional atmosphere between you. Is it better or worse? Do you feel closer or more estranged? Did you glean any new insights or information? What would help things resolve? An apology, a hug, a handshake, a salute? Perhaps agreeing to disagree and part ways? Sometimes agreeing not to be in contact is a positive resolution. Whatever it is, do it now in your imagination. See the resolution in your mind's eye.

Now say goodbye and watch the other person walk away. Check and see if you feel different after they have left. What did you learn about yourself, your 'opponent', and the conflict?

You can also use this exercise to work on unresolved feelings from past abuses, regrets and conflicts. Unfinished business from the past burdens our hearts, making it harder to be with our loved ones in present time. It impedes our sense of trust and openness in the here and now. Very often these were past events in which we were unable to take our own side or defend ourselves, or where, because we were unable to see the other side, we possibly hurt others. These events continue to haunt us and eat at our self-esteem. If you find yourself still angry, sad or upset about events in the past, it may be time to resolve them through inner work. Working on these events inside ourselves can lead to new power, pride and self-knowledge.

Forgiving old conflicts: Looking deeply and understanding

Sometimes we have a conflict from the past that haunts us. We just can't resolve it for ourselves. Very often, the person who was involved is no longer in our lives, or the conflict just seems irresolvable. In these cases, we can always attempt to resolve the matter within ourselves by forgiving the person and ourselves. By working internally on these unhappy conflicts, as with all conflicts, we can learn how to handle similar situations in the future. We can learn when to retreat from conflict, when to go forward, and when to get help from other people such as a mediator or therapist. The following is a brief internal exercise to help you work through an outer conflict.

Exercise: Looking deeply
You may need to do this exercise several times before you feel it taking hold. Take as long as you need to do the exercise.
1. Lie or sit comfortably.
2. See the person in your mind's eye. Say hello and acknowledge the conflict that exists between you.
3. Ask them what was it that you didn't understand about them or the situation. Now look and listen deeply for the answer. Accept it. Now tell them what it was they didn't

understand about you. Watch them take in this new understanding. Thank each other for being willing to look and
listen deeply.

4. See yourself look into each other's eyes for a moment. Say
goodbye and watch them leave.

5. Ask God, the Universe, Nature or your Higher Self to help
complete the healing. Then let it go.

6. What did you learn from this encounter? What do you
understand now that you didn't before?

Projection: Me in you and you in me

It is an axiom of modern psychology that we project the
disowned parts of ourselves onto our partners, our friends, and
even strangers, who have 'terrible' or 'wonderful' characteristics
we deny in ourselves. For instance, we may always end up in
relationships with partners who have awful tempers, though we
consider ourselves reasonable and mild-mannered. If this is the
case, it may be time to consider the possibility we are denying
our own power or anger. Denying our power or anger, the
energy we need to assert our needs and defend ourselves, has
the unfortunate effect of leaving us vulnerable to the power or
anger of others. As we claim our power, we will find ourselves
choosing different kinds of partners and friends.

Our tendency to project our disowned qualities onto others
is often related to unfinished business with our family of
origin. We tend to see our significant others as exhibiting the
same qualities as our parent or caretaker who was most difficult
(or wonderful) for us. We project these same qualities onto
others and then relate to these people as we did to our original

parent or caretaker – with meekness, subservience, rebellion, blame, adoration or fear. Projection happens to some extent in virtually all intimate relationships. It can happen between friends or co-workers too. We are often attracted to people who express parts of our selves we can't fully own or have yet to grow into.

Projection is a deep and complex issue and beyond the scope of this book. For readers who are interested in learning more about this topic, I recommend the book *Intimate Partners* by Maggie Scarf. She says that conflict between people is really a conflict in our own heads; that is, with our own projection. Owning and taking responsibility for those parts of ourselves we prefer to project on to others can greatly reduce many unproductive fights. Conflict is more productive and gratifying when you are actually fighting about real issues and not simply fighting your own projected parts – the inner rejection of your own anger, weakness, dependency or need for control.

Ellen, a client of mine, consistently tells me that she is attracted to dominating extroverts, and has a terrible time holding her own with them, being quite shy and introverted herself. Why does she torture herself like this? She unconsciously desires the freedom to express herself more assertively. Her partners, more often than not, crave the rich inner life she has cultivated in herself.

Ellen is gradually learning to assert herself verbally by sheer necessity of living with her 'pushy' partners. Her father was controlling and dominating, and so she continues to feel controlled and dominated by her powerful partners. Her most recent partner was a woman and, to her disappointment, she found the pattern continued, even with someone of the same gender. As she worked on this problem and slowly built up her own sense of power, learning to stand up for her side, three curious things happened. First, her eighteen-year-old daughter decided it was time to live with her father for a while, freeing Ellen, a single mother, from being the primary caretaker for the first time in many years. Second, she was offered a more powerful position at work, a position she felt required her to be more outgoing than she was. With support, she took the job and found she was more than a match for it. Third, she met and fell in love with a woman of a totally different nature from her other partners, someone as gentle as herself.

Usually when we work on integrating into ourselves the qualities we have projected onto our partner, our partners change too, or else we find ourselves in a relationship that is less polarised and more compatible. As we find balance within, we find balance without. As we accept the totality of our being (both the wonderful and not-so-wonderful qualities), we take more responsibility for our lives and the lessons we receive.

Refusing false projections

While it is important to own those parts of yourself that you project onto others, it is also important to stop others from projecting their problems onto you.

Story: Nancy trusts her own perceptions

Nancy was a woman who felt emotionally abused by her female boss. Her boss was a very powerful woman, well respected in the business community, but she was also harsh and critical at times. She took a dislike to Nancy and began projecting all manner of faults upon her, saying she was sloppy, disorganised and disrespectful. I knew for a fact that Nancy was extremely conscientious, polite, gracious, highly organised, professional and open-minded. But perhaps due to her gracious and open disposition, she had a tendency to take on other people's opinions of her, whether true or false. She *believed* the negative projections her boss was placing on her and tortured herself with them.

I helped Nancy to reject these toxic projections and to affirm her wonderful nature. She began to distinguish toxic feedback from constructive feedback and to see when someone's perceptions of her were valid or when they were not.

The key for Nancy was learning to trust her *own* perceptions. When someone gave her feedback, she learned to check inside to see if it rang true for her. If so, she could safely assume the feedback was mostly accurate. But if the feedback made her feel crazy, disoriented or bad about herself, as the feedback from her boss did, she was to assume the feedback was wrong for her, that it was a toxic projection. Nancy was also to take careful note of the nonverbal communication that accompanied any feedback, such as voice tone, eye contact and body language, to help her gauge whether the feedback was constructive or destructive.

After deciding that her boss was not good for her health, Nancy resigned and found herself another job. While hunting for a job she paid extra care to the vibrations she felt from the interviewer or potential boss. If the interaction allowed her to feel at ease, confident and able to speak, she was to assume the person was able to 'see' her. If she felt blocked, unable to speak, frozen or small, she was to assume the interaction was one in which she was not able to be 'seen'. In this way, she learned an important lesson about the power of projection and the need to carefully examine the impact of others' perceptions upon her.

Exercise: Inner conflict

1. Describe an inner conflict you have, some issue or tension spot within you.
2. Try to differentiate the conflict into two sides or voices.
3. Give each side a name. Help them converse with each other. Sometimes writing down the dialogue helps them to speak.
4. Listen for any inequality between the sides. Does one side sound more dominant, loud, sure? Whose voice does this remind you of? How does the other side sound? If one side sounds weaker, help it to express itself more fully.
5. Ask yourself, 'Which side sounds like my *deepest* self, my deepest desire?'
6. Help the two sides come to a negotiated agreement as to a way forward.
7. Step out and take the neutral side if you get stuck, and take a look at what is happening. Where are things stuck? Does one side need to take its side more? Is one side refusing to listen to the other?
8. Continue the dialogue until you learn something new about yourself. What did you learn? How do you feel about the issue now?

Thoughts to hold

- Inner conflict creates tension within us and can lead to physical symptoms.
- Inner conflict usually has two sides or point of view that are warring in our heads.
- Listen carefully to what both sides have to say. Give each side a name.
- Each side is important and has information for you.
- Cultivate a Fair Witness within that can listen and support both sides, and help you take the neutral side and find resolution.
- It is important to let go of conflicts that are old and irresolvable.
- Some conflicts with others are about our own projections. We can resolve them by reclaiming the projection.
- We can avoid taking on other people's toxic projections by developing our own side more.

11 Domestic Hot Spots:
Housework, Money and Sex

If we do not change our direction, we are likely to end up where we are headed.

Ancient Chinese Proverb

At the root of many intimate relationship battles are chronic and sometimes deadly power struggles. Some of the deadliest are over housework, money and sex. These can be inflammatory topics and are undeniably the top three issues in many relationships. For this reason I have dedicated a whole chapter to these three topics.

1. Housework horrors

A young woman named Maria worked with me on the issue of housework in her marriage. For Maria, doing the housework was an expression of love for her husband, which he appeared to take for granted. As a result she deeply resented it. She felt unloved by his refusal to do housework. I helped her separate the issue of love from the issue of housework and suggested she didn't make it a love issue but a fairness issue. After all, they both loved each other but neither of them enjoyed housework.

Her husband, in an effort to resolve the conflict, had even suggested she give him a list of chores to do each week but she resisted doing this because she felt she would still be in the role of mother dispensing duties. If he loved her, he would just clean up, wouldn't he?

Maria had a hard time letting go of the housework because she wanted it done a certain way. After working through her feelings about her need to let go of the 'Mother' role, we came up with the idea that they devise a weekly list together over a cup of tea and biscuits. The lists were to be reasonable and not too laborious. Once the lists were divided she was to let go of everything but her designated half. Now clear about her side she went home with renewed hope for this problem. Her husband gladly agreed to this proposal. In order for this solution to stick, Maria had to abide by her side of the agreement and not criticise his way of cleaning. She needed to accept that sometimes the house would not look exactly the way she wanted it to. That's life. If ever there was an issue that requires compromise, it's housework. One side usually needs to do less and be less exacting, and the other side usually needs to do more and be more conscientious. At stake are issues of fairness. Perhaps both sides need to do less or do more together.

There is a new gender contract slowly emerging based on equality. It requires a deep degree of social change that will only show results over time. It's important not to take some of these seemingly entrenched conflicts between men and women, such as housework, too personally. These types of conflicts are widespread throughout society.

I have no pat answer to the problems of equity in housework and domestic caring. Each relationship and household will need to explore the issues, using a constructive approach such as the model of conflict resolution used in this book.

Other side of the story: Domesticity and Jane's compulsion to clean up

Jane is a warm, bright woman in her early fifties who has been divorced for twenty years. She's had several short-term relationships since. She told me she felt afraid of confrontation and becomes spaced out and disconnected during conflict. For example, she once offered her opinion on a particular topic to her ex-boyfriend. He said, 'You talk too much'. Immediately she fell into an altered state: she stared off into space and smiled vacuously, nodding her head like one of those ornamental dogs in the back of cars. She could not respond; she could only cope in the only way she knew how – to act like everything was okay. She was 'gone'. Sometimes, it only takes one comment to throw us off centre.

When we worked on this conflict, I told Jane to smile and nod the way she did in the original situation. I repeated the words her boyfriend had said to her: 'You talk too much'. She went into a mini-trance. When I asked her to describe her inner experience, she said she felt as if she were in an empty, silent, white room. I asked Jane what her body was doing while she stared zombie-like into the white room. She said her mind was vacant but her body felt fidgety and restless. I asked her to continue fidgeting. To my surprise, she got up and began rearranging the books on my shelf and straightening the tassels on my rug. She said that when confronted with something difficult or hurtful, she withdraws and tidies her house. She was a compulsive house cleaner.

Her house was immaculate but her relationships were messy. What was happening to Jane?

One part of Jane was paralysed and stuck, symbolised visually as a empty white room. This part of Jane felt helpless as she stared fixedly and smiled vacuously. Yet another part of Jane was agitated and felt compelled to move and clean up. I asked her to keep cleaning and to study herself as she did so. She cleaned up for a while and then suddenly stopped and said, as if finally understanding her actions, 'I'm creating order out of chaos!' I asked her if she had a name for this ordering part of herself. After a moment, she said, 'Worthy'. I was surprised and asked her to tell me a story about this name.

Jane said that for a long time when she first became a businesswoman she felt as if she were 'faking' her competence and hiding the true mess she was deep inside. Then one day she realised that she really *was* a competent person, and she felt *worthy* after all. That had been a pivotal moment for Jane.

Jane's inner conflict about how straightforward she could be in relationship had kept her stuck in unhelpful and passive behaviour in her intimate relationships. Raised by a critical mother, she had learned to internalise other people's opinions of her and to keep silent. When Jane's new boyfriend told her she talked too much, she felt immobilised, just as she did when criticised as a child. She cleaned the house. Doing the housework can be an escape mechanism or tension release valve. It can be used positively or negatively as a way to manage tension.

I told Jane to imagine herself in the original conflict with her former boyfriend and see herself as this worthy self, the one who could take charge and create order. I suggested she use this skill to clean up the emotional mess between them. She paused for a moment and then said to the imaginary partner, 'Why do you put me down and say I talk too much after I have given my opinion? I feel sad that you need to be mean to me.' She sighed a sigh of relief. She had said what she had not been able to say before. It was so simple yet so difficult, due to her belief that she shouldn't confront others. She felt great at having finally taken her own side. Her impulse to express herself directly was buried within her compulsion to clean up.

I thought it unfortunate that Jane had not been able to take her own side when she was with this man, and so had left him. Had they known how, Jane and her friend might have embarked on a conversation that could have enriched their relationship. When we cannot take our own side in a situation, we often leave as a way of resolving the tension. This is an indirect way of taking of our own side and is unfortunately often the only way we know how to express ourselves.

Jane found the key to unlocking her frozen state by studying her own behaviour. The keys to our freedom are always within us. In Jane's case, the key to unlocking her frozen state was through observing her fidgety body movements and her desire to clean up my room. She realised that *setting the house straight* felt safer than *being straight* in relationship.

The image of domesticity in Jane's process was an interesting one, given women's traditional role as cleaner and caretaker. Women have always cleaned up the physical mess of others: the housework. These ancient skills of cleaning, mending, and ordering can be transferred to cleaning up interpersonal messes in communication. We clean up our relationships by bringing attention to issues and working through them together.

Don't pretend everything is 'clean' when it isn't. Don't run and do the dishes when you get upset. Do the conflict. Making sure things are clean and straight between you is ultimately more important than the kitchen sink. As a woman writer once said, if you want to lead a creative life, stop doing the housework!

I know many busy working couples that pitch in together to clean the house once a fortnight for two hours straight, going at it great guns. It's a chore, after all, for most people. Their house may not look utterly spick and span from day to day, but they're too busy leading their deeper lives to care.

Exercise: Cleaning up the house together

1. Think of a conflict you have or have had with someone about housework. What is the main issue? Does the other side do too little or too much cleaning? Do you? Who initiated the conflict and why?
2. Now let yourself look more deeply into your side of the issue. If you're someone who likes to have a very clean home and wants others to want that too, think about why this is so important to you. Or, if you like a more relaxed and casual home and want others to want that too, think about why this is so important to you. Imagine the kind of home you want to live in. How does it look? What is its character or atmosphere? How is it cleaned and maintained?
3. Imagine the other side talking about what kind of home they want to live in and why.
4. When you understand the type of home each of you want

and why, see where your visions are similar or dissimilar.

5. Brainstorm together about how the housework can be handled in a way that respects each person's vision, makes both sides happy, and is fair and equitable. Come up with a list of options to choose from. You may want to change options periodically to see which works best.

2. Money is a major issue

Differences over money are vastly underrated as a source of conflict. Money tensions can create enormous strain in relationships and are often cited as the main reason for couples breaking up.

I once worked with a couple on their money issues. The husband had inherited a large sum of money and no longer needed to work for a living (a very complex and not always desirable happenstance). His younger wife was barely making it in her photography business. He owned the house, and she lived with him rent-free. For this she was expected to cook, clean and shop, as well as work fulltime. The problem with this contract was that it didn't address the fact that money matters cannot be resolved by using only a logical dollar and cents computation. What was missing was an understanding of how his money gave him great power to call the shots.

Neither of them grasped the power dynamic between them. As a result, she became deeply resentful about having to do all the housework when she worked fulltime and he worked not at all. Deep down he believed that women rip men off; therefore he expected his partner to work for her keep (rent), even though he never earned his fortune at all but had inherited it.

The wife often failed to complete her household tasks, angering him further. They cycled this way for many months with her feeling resentful and failing at her side of the deal. He felt ripped off and angry. At the end of a very bitter battle, they decided to separate. This case showed me once again that money issues need to be addressed not only as a maths problem but also as an emotional and psychological dilemma.

Interestingly, after they separated, the young wife started to do very well in her career.

Why is money such a big issue?

Money represents power and freedom in our society. We often attribute all kinds of qualities to someone who has a lot of money, such as wisdom, strength, intelligence, judgment and authority.

Though strides have been made, women are still at a disadvantage when it comes to money. Some women are extremely successful today and earn more than their male partners, but very often, women still lag behind men when it comes to financial security, income and assets. This financial differential can create a sense of insecurity, dependency or inferiority in women. In addition, women can feel guilty if they are not as financially successful as their men, nor as financially independent. They blame themselves for not being more aggressive in the world or for expecting men to look after them.

The good news is that women are learning to take control of their financial lives and are learning how to invest and build wealth. They are slowly gaining momentum financially and mastering this most male of provinces. Some of the wealthiest people in the world are women. Women's investment clubs outperform all other investment clubs, including mixed and all-male. When women decide to harness their power together and generate prosperity with the support of other women, they are unstoppable.

Money and the changing gender contract

Today's couples are faced with the task of creating unique fiscal contracts that work for them. Even if a woman and man do prefer the old gender contract in which the man earns the money and the woman takes charge of the domestic sphere, this is increasingly difficult to manage, as economic changes make survival on one income impossible for many families. But whatever the fiscal arrangement between couples, the fact remains that many women are still vulnerable to low-status, low-paying jobs with slow promotions. Many women feel desperate and afraid of not being able to gain financial control of their lives. Sometimes the situation is reversed with the woman earning the lion's share of the household income. This can be hard on a man who was raised to think of himself as the main provider and to derive masculine self-esteem from this task. Even in same-gender couples, there can be a primary income earner, generating similar issues to those between a heterosexual couple.

Children present another money issue. Child rearing often means staying home and depending on partners to provide financially, or else paying child-care costs. Many women who stayed at home to raise children and run a household, expecting to be supported by their husbands, have found themselves in mid-life divorced, penniless and unskilled for the labour force. These displaced homemakers are thrown into a crisis they never expected. As the traditional gender contract becomes obsolete, there are many casualties left behind. Financial parity with men is a goal still to be realised. ·

Family of origin

As well as the immediate differences in real dollars between people, each of us bring entrenched money attitudes from our family backgrounds. We learn about money from our original family. These family of origin money attitudes influence our behaviour towards money. Some of us like to 'live it up', while others are thrifty and cautious. Some of us were given a sound financial education while others do not have the knowledge we need to create financial stability in our lives. These differing background experiences can create conflict in a relationship until they are discussed and understood.

Talking about money can be hard to do

Many of us were raised not to discuss money openly. It is often a painful issue to discuss because it brings up feelings of dependency, resentment, shame, constriction, lack of freedom, and other pressures and burdens. Most people don't like to admit how much they have, or how little. But regardless of how much or how little each of us earns, it is important to not let this fact silence us or rob us of our decision-making power in relationship. But it often does. As everyone knows, the one with the money often has the final say in decision-making. But we should be extremely careful about becoming hypnotised by money-power in our relationships or surrendering our own personal power when we have less money than our partner. Feeling dependent on someone for our physical survival can have a deadly impact. Some women hesitate to speak openly in their relationship because they fear rejection. Rejection could mean having to survive on their own, which they don't feel ready to do.

Paying for things sometimes allows men – and women also – to feel they don't have to deal with emotional issues in relationship, that they are 'giving enough already'. This should never be used as a reason to avoid working on issues that impede intimacy. I have seen women bring up a legitimate complaint to their financially stronger partner only to be reminded by the partner that they are 'paying for them'. That usually has the effect of silencing the woman. Don't be silenced by the money-card: if this happens to you, let your partner know that you realise money *is* an important topic to discuss, and assure them that you will discuss it with them later, but not to divert your complaint by trumping it with the money-card.

Some people find talking about money, as with sex, *indelicate.* The hands-off attitude may have been workable in the days when sex roles were rigidly determined and everyone knew their place, but it is not tenable in today's world of shifting roles and large-scale economic changes. Now more than ever, women need to be talking about money, the way it impacts their individual lives and especially how it impacts their behaviour and feelings in their relationships with others.

We must talk about money

With the current high divorce rate, we can't afford *not* to talk about money and its effect on a relationship. The feelings that money brings up need to be discussed gently together so that solutions can be found that provide an adequate sense of security *and* autonomy for both individuals. These solutions will have to be revisited often as conditions and needs change.

It is wise to approach the money issue as soon as possible in a committed relationship. And it usually needs to be addressed on an ongoing basis. Discrepancies in income, family inheritances, material assets, sense of freedom to buy things or make money decisions should all be addressed. Though there may be no immediate practical solution to the discrepancies in income or assets, the *feelings* about these discrepancies can be dealt with in a safe atmosphere.

We need to talk about money. We need to discuss our different attitudes and expectations and talk frankly about differences in financial privilege and means. Couples should discuss ways to equalise the sense of empowerment in decision-making if there are disparities in financial resources. Having a voice and a vote is always to be encouraged. Both partners need to educate themselves about money and become knowledgeable about money management, investing, budgets, balance sheets and taxes.

Story: Exploring financial differences

Beth and Stephen fell in love at first sight and married after a year of dating. They moved in together after the marriage and faced the task of putting a household together and figuring out how to share resources. Stephen had quite a bit more income than Beth, who was just making ends meet in her job as a hair stylist. Stephen agreed to support them until Beth got on her feet.

One day they went shopping in the supermarket together. As they shopped, Beth noticed that Stephen threw into the cart whatever items he liked, but whenever Beth did the same, he inspected the item for price to see whether or not it was too expensive. Beth felt shamed by this, and resigned herself to walking behind Stephen in the supermarket like a child eyeing goods but not daring to touch. She couldn't bear Stephen's rejection of her choices. Stephen had become the official money decision-maker. When they got home, Beth burst into tears and confessed that she found this state of affairs humiliating. Stephen was surprised. He had not noticed her pain in the market and thought he was more than generous. Thus began a process of discussing money in the relationship and the baggage both brought to the table.

Stephen's father had given up his dreams of going to medical school to become an insurance salesman and support the family. Deep down, Stephen was terrified of the same thing happening to him: giving up his dreams to support others. Beth's mother had been a housewife who always used to snap at Beth whenever she needed something, 'Ask you father. It's *his* money!' Beth was terrified of becoming dependent on a man for money and was afraid to come clean about her debts and/or to ask for help.

All these fears had to be discussed. It involved vulnerability and sharing. But Stephen and Beth sat down and began to talk. They were pleased with themselves because they had broken a big taboo: they had talked about money and the impact of money on their individual lives and their life together.

Eventually they set up a joint account, as well as keeping their own separate accounts. They estimated their joint rent, food and utility costs for a month and put in that amount each month into the account. At first, Stephen put in most of the money, but as Beth got on her feet, she put in more each month. She had a goal to shoot for. Stephen was happy that they had a workable plan and did not feel saddled anymore with an unspoken sense that he should take care of all the finances forever. He knew she was working towards her goal and also realised he had issues to look at too, even though he had more money.

Stephen realised that having more money didn't make him a better decision-maker, necessarily. He realised that what he needed was for Beth to help him with the emotional weight of paying for things and with planning their financial life together. He wanted her to take control of paying the bills, decide about investments, and help carry the mental stress. He didn't want to be left alone to bear the weight of fiscal responsibility.

Money was an issue they continued to address on a regular basis; not just the facts and figures, but also the feelings, attitudes and unspoken needs, and how these were impacting on their relationship.

Exercise: Talking about money

How to approach prickly money issues? First of all, try talking about money using the four steps of conflict resolution described in Chapters 3 to 6. Pick a time, place and topic and thoroughly explore the issue.

Here is a sample list of money topics to choose from. See which of these topics prick your attention.

Income: What do we each earn?

Cashflow: Income versus expenses?

Assets: Savings, property, investments?

Background attitudes: How were you raised?

Insurance: What's covered? What does it cost?

Credit cards: How much debt?

Individual needs: How do they get covered?

Allowances: How much should the kids get?

Taxes: Who pays them and how much?

Loans: Whose are they and how much?

Self-esteem: Confidence in handling money?

Inequality: Facing the pain of money disparities?

Security: Retirement, investments, home?

Inheritances: What can we expect?

Knowledge: How does one build wealth?

Bills: Who pays them?

Bookkeeping: Who does the chequebooks?

Decisions: How do purchases get decided?

Luxuries: Eating out, travel, presents?

Power: Do we work as a peer-team or hierarchy?

Financial privacy: How much do we need?

Trust: Can we share our money?

Money values: Goals, ethics, and beliefs?

Identity: Male/female money role expectations?

3. Sex: The underground conflict

Sex is hard to talk about, too

Like money, sex is hard to talk about for most people. People will fight relatively happily about who does the dishes (also a legitimate topic) but when it comes to sex, 'mum's the word'. Most people long to be open about their feelings and needs with their partner, how they like to be touched during sex, but feel too shy or insecure to say so. It is embarrassing and awkward and we don't want our partner to get hurt. Or, in some cases, sex becomes a battleground with each person blaming the other for the lack of frequency or joy in sex. Handling sexual conflicts with negativity, blame and judgment can destroy a sexual relationship.

Along with this tendency to be silent about sex, sex itself often becomes the battleground for non-sexual matters, hurts and power-struggles that have yet to be articulated or resolved. Contrary to popular opinion, women are not the only ones who withhold sex. Men too may avoid and withhold sex in intimate relationships. Many relationships die sexually because background angers and issues are not being dealt with. The build-up of repressed tension and hostility turns everyone off, resulting in sexual rejection. Resolving our conflicts is usually good for our sex lives.

Exploring sexual differences

Many people are awkward or shy when it comes to discussing intimate details about their preferences in bed, especially in long-term relationships where we have so many non-sexual issues with our partner, as well as sexual ones. Here's an example of how people don't always say what they mean even when they think they do.

Story: Kevin and Rose learn to court

Kevin and Rose are a married couple in their late twenties. They had been married for seven years and loved each other dearly but couldn't seem to ever have sex any more. Rose felt too shy to initiate sex. Kevin felt burdened by the pressure to initiate all the time and had consequently gone on strike. He loved Rose but disliked what he saw as her passivity. They had talked about it many times but it never seemed to resolve.

Like many couples, their relationship suffered from tensions around sex. They had developed a kind of physical intimacy stalemate. Kevin felt resentful. Rose was hurt by Kevin's lack of interest in her sexually. They were locked in a power struggle about who would initiate. They blamed each other for being inadequate. They battled on for two years with both of them feeling badly about themselves and each other.

It all blew up one day when Kevin had a brief affair. After the affair, Kevin knew he wanted to make things work with Rose, that he did love her after all. He decided to tell her the truth. He came home and confessed to Rose what he had done. Rose was furious and hurt, but relieved he had told her. They decided to stay together and learn how to better meet their intimacy needs.

Once again, Kevin tried to explain that he felt Rose neglected him sexually. Rose said that when she did initiate sex, he didn't respond. Instead of getting defensive, he asked her what she meant, *which he hadn't done before*. She said he just lay there, still and quiet. What was he supposed to do? he wondered. 'Show you like it,' said Rose. 'Like women do', she added. 'You know, make sounds, squirm or move a bit, show your pleasure to me.' A light bulb went on in his head. That is what she meant by respond – showing his pleasure.

Now he understood what she was saying. Kevin was shy in that department – making noises and being expressive sexually did not come naturally to him. He was unaware that his quietness in bed was an issue until that moment. Though they had talked about sex in the past, somehow this detail hadn't emerged. Rose hadn't taken her side all the way. She hadn't expressed everything. She had been too shy to come out with her side, too scared to upset the apple cart.

Kevin and Rose saw where they got stuck: he was reluctant to show her his pleasure so she was reluctant to initiate contact. In other words, Rose needed more positive responses from Kevin when she initiated sexual contact. She interpreted his quietness as negative feedback to what she was doing. She needed clearly visible signs from him to keep going. They also made another discovery. They realised they had married very quickly and had gone straight into a full sexual relationship. They had never gone through the process of courting and making-out and exploring foreplay together, which both of them wanted and needed to create a relaxing and intimate atmosphere for sex. They began practising just cuddling and kissing on the sofa without pressure to rush into intercourse. They were learning how to truly communicate about sex.

Often we think we have communicated everything, but it takes a process of unfolding each side until our deeper needs have been articulated in specific detail. We often skip over the specifics and stay with the general, using such terms as 'respond' or 'initiate' without saying what we really mean.

Sometimes it takes a crisis for people to be willing to open up. If we work on our tensions, we can sometimes prevent crisis. However, crisis can be a wake up call that can have a healing and cleansing effect. Using conflict resolution can make the most out of these stressful times.

Sex can be discussed like everything else. A friend once pithily pointed out that there are only three issues in sex: doing it too little, doing it too much, or doing it with the wrong person. Like all conflict, sexual conflicts usually revolve around people wanting more or less of something. This may sound cold but actually it is supportive of both partners getting their needs met and learning about what makes the other happy, rather than guessing and hoping to get it right. Honesty leads to satisfaction in and out of bed.

Two ways to approach sex conflicts

1. **Focus on other issues first:** There are two main ways to approach conflicts over sex. The first is to explore whether the conflict is not about sex at all but about some other aspect of the relationship that's not working well, such as struggles for power and control, money issues, survival or work-related tensions and stresses, lack of privacy or independence, emotional hurts, or destructive dynamics such as resentment, jealousy, lack of fairness or equity.

   Often sexual conflicts come down to one of two non-sexual dynamics in a relationship: either too much distance in a relationship or more likely, too much closeness – in other words, not enough space, independence, respect and individuality. Here's a tip: love loves democracy and justice. That's why most books on conflict between couples suggest that if a man wants more sex in his relationship he should try mopping the kitchen floor or washing the dishes! Justice, fairness and equity are powerful aphrodisiacs.

2. **Focus on sexuality in the relationship:** If exploring non-sexual issues has failed to help a sexual conflict, it's time to focus directly on the sexual relationship between you. If you go down this path, you need to set up the conversation so that both people feel safe and respected. Remember, sexuality is just about the most private aspect of a person. You can't get much more personal than that. So proceed with caution. Why I advocate this cautionary approach to sexual conflicts is that hurtful things said in this area often remain with people for a long time and damages their sense of sexual confidence with each other. There are many good books available on sexual issues in a relationship. A good place to start is *Passionate Marriage* by David Schnarch. Educate yourself about this type of conflict before wading into deep waters. The vagaries and mysteries of sexual chemistry are perplexing to most people, so treat each other with sensitivity and care.

Talking about sex

So, how do we go about talking about sex, presuming that is the path we choose to go down? How do we deal with the inevitable sexual differences that arise between people? I have no sure-fire answer to that ancient dilemma but I do recommend approaching these differences using the four-step conflict resolution procedure described in Chapters 3 to 6.

First of all, choose a specific issue and agree to discuss it in a safe place and at a good time for both of you. We need to create a safe space to discuss sex, as it can be scary to do so, especially when things aren't going well. Plan the discussion in advance so both of you have time to mentally prepare, limiting the discussion to a time period, say forty minutes. Choosing a particular issue such as frequency, lack of desire, fairness, oral sex or satisfaction, can help minimise the anxiety. Then proceed as you would any other topic. Take your side, take theirs, and take the neutral perspective. And stay focused on learning and understanding each other. You don't have to solve the problem overnight; it will help to simply begin to understand more about what is happening between you.

Engaging in conflict resolution about sex can be enormously informative. Be very careful not to use any dirty fighting tactics. This is especially crucial for sex conflicts. You need to be impeccable here, as the potential to wound each other is great. For instance, it can be a dirty fighting tactic to say, 'And we haven't had sex in months!' when you are in the middle of discussing other issues. Sex is best not combined with other topics. Ideally, sex conflicts should be discussed separately.

If talking about sex is too difficult to do, or if the nature of the sexual problem stems from a traumatic sexual event, such as rape or childhood sexual abuse, ask a therapist to facilitate the process. Always get help when you are unable to deal with an issue by yourself. Sexual issues are often an area where people need outside help.

To get you started, here's a sample list of discussion points:

Touch: How do I want to be touched?

Talking: What do I like to say or hear?

Where: Best locations?

Duration: How long is best?

Orgasm: What works for me?

Differences: Expectations, beliefs and habits?

Time: Best times?

Frequency: How often?

Others: Expectations around fidelity?

Foreplay: How to do it? What works best?

Mood helpers: Lights, music, food, oils?

Pornography: Should it be allowed or used?

Safe sex: Knowing and applying the rules?

Avoidance: What are we resisting?

Desire: What feeds it?

Knowledge: Need to know more about sex?

Flirting with others: What's okay?

Initiating: How to share the responsibility?

Sexual trauma: Has there been hurt?

Contraception: What's fair and safe?

Fears: What are our insecurities?

Other conflicts: Other issues are impacting sex?

Exercise: Using a gentle touch with sex conflicts

This exercise gives you an opportunity to explore a sexual conflict and to practice expressing your side and hearing theirs without judgment or blame.

1. Think of a conflict you have or have had with someone about sex.
2. What is your side? What is the essence of what you need?
3. How can you say this without judging or blaming the other side?
4. Imagine what the other side would say in return.
5. How can you support their viewpoint without feeling criticised? Can you accept their side?

6. Step out and take the neutral side. What do you see? What is needed to restore peace and understanding?

7. What have you learned from this conversation? How can you apply what you learned?

Thoughts to hold

- Housework, money and sex are three of the biggest conflict areas in intimate relationships.
- Housework is an area where compromise is often needed.
- Unequal divisions of labour over housework can cause relationships to break down.
- Differences in income or wealth between people can create subtle or overt power struggles.
- It is important to discuss the ways money impacts on our feelings and behaviour in relationships.
- Feeling dependent financially can make it hard to take your own side.
- Sexuality is a sensitive issue for most people. Never use dirty fighting tactics when discussing sex.
- Non-sexual issues that aren't addressed can create sexual problems in a relationship.
- Differences in money and sexuality are opportunities to know and love one another more deeply.

12 Clean and Dirty Fighting

We are all part of the Great Holy Mystery – all of us –
and so we can't hate each other or we are hating ourselves.

Anonymous

Many of us don't know how to conflict well because we were never taught effective and loving methods. In fact, many of us learned to *fight dirty* as children. We observed our care-givers, teachers and siblings using insults and name-calling, being angry and blaming. In the school playground we learned that might equals right and that revenge is justified. Many women learned to avoid conflict by lying and manipulating – these are all 'dirty fighting' techniques.

No wonder we can feel frustrated and hopeless about ever resolving conflict. It is not helpful, however, to blame ourselves for not knowing better. In fact, we need to forgive ourselves for using tactics that may have caused pain for ourselves and others.

Dirty versus clean fighting

Dirty fighting tactics involve trying to win or overpower the other side. We blame others, criticise and judge them, call them names, and try to tarnish their good image. We seek revenge and get caught in keeping score of injuries. We are also fighting dirty when we act defensive and guarded and withhold information, and when we refuse to take responsibility for our actions or face a hard truth about ourselves.

Dirty fighters like to make threats and demands. They like to ambush others and pick fights at inappropriate times. Dirty fighting is wounding and potentially deadly. It creates resentment and leaves emotional scars.

Dirty fighting is about revenge. It is about getting back at others because we have been hurt. It is about power and insecurity rather than understanding or connection. Dirty fighting destroys relationships.

We all use dirty fighting tactics from time to time, and women are just as guilty of it as men. In fact, with women's well developed verbal skills, we can be astonishingly destructive at verbally ripping the other side to shreds. What is the alternative? The alternative is to fight clean. Clean fighting means training ourselves to conflict differently.

Clean fighting is about communicating honestly and directly. Clean fighters do not try to win at the other's expense but do present their side clearly and strongly. They concede when the other side makes a good point, and never take swipes at another's weak spot. They do not dominate the conversation, nor do they criticise how the other is expressing their side. They do not blame others and try not to judge. Clean fighters feel secure enough in themselves to be able to apologise, admit mistakes and listen to the other side. They are committed to working things out fairly, and value others as they value themselves.

Clean fighting	Dirty fighting
• Respects the other's integrity	• Name-calls and insults
• Wants to resolve the problem	• Wants to win
• Is direct and honest	• Is indirect and manipulative
• Stays with the present issue	• Drags up incidents from past
• Commits to completing the process	• Leaves or withdraws
• Expresses needs and feelings	• Uses sarcasm
• Is direct with anger and criticisms	• Punishes, threatens and blames
• Owns mistakes and limits	• Denies responsibility
• Gives equal space to both sides	• Dominates and controls the space
• Can forgive	• Is vengeful
• Understands both sides are learning	• Is intolerant of mistakes
• Plans a good time for discussion	• Ambushes conflict partner
• Tries not to harm	• Goes for vulnerable spot
• Is specific and detailed	• Is vague and general
• Points out dirty fighting	• Allows dirty fighting to happen
• Speaks for self only	• Assumes knows what the other is thinking

Commit to fighting clean now

Conflict resolution is about letting go of dirty fighting tactics and adopting clean ones. One of the main reasons people avoid conflict is because they fear that dirty fighting tactics will be employed. No conflict is ever resolved using dirty fighting tactics. When it comes to conflict resolution, the means and the end are the same. Good resolutions come from using good conflict tactics: respect, honesty, patience and willingness to learn.

Commit now to fighting clean. We do that by becoming aware of our behaviour and the impact it has on others and ourselves. We commit to breaking the cycle of revenge, letting go of controlling the outcome, and striving for understanding. These three components of clean fighting can be summed up as: Don't hurt back, accept the outcome, and learn from the result.

1. Don't hurt back

The most important commitment we can make to fight clean is to refrain from acting out our impulse for revenge. People say and do things that hurt us. That's life. We become clean fighters when we recognise our hurt and make a conscious choice not to hurt back. We can express our pain, even our honest anger. We can ask for an apology. We can stand up for ourselves. But we do not say or do anything to intentionally injure the other side. The other side may feel hurt if we express our feelings, but we do not try to hurt them. Not one little dig. Not one indirect swipe. Can you resist this? It can be difficult. But that is clean fighting.

My mentor used to say that revenge is the grease on the wheels of history. This means that we all keep the cycle of revenge going every time we 'hit back' at someone. Clean fighting means we stop the cycle of revenge. It is a tall order and sometimes we slip, but that is a commitment we make to ourselves and to the world.

We can and must object when others try to hurt us with their dirty fighting tactics, but we don't use dirty fighting tactics in return. It may give us a momentary sense of satisfaction, but it will create more conflict in our lives in the long run. By committing to fighting clean we slowly reduce the amount of inner and outer conflict in our lives. We will resolve our old conflicts and not create new ones. We will break the cycle of revenge.

2. Accept the outcome

Another commitment we can make to clean fighting, and it is above all a commitment, is to practise accepting the outcome. By this I do not mean abandoning our own side or giving up on trying to improve things or find solutions. I mean accepting the outcome of the conflict for now. We may not be able to change things overnight. We may not be able to make someone hear or understand our side. We may not get what we want immediately.

Accepting the outcome means that we do our best to solve things and then we accept what happens next. We do not use force to control the outcome to get our way. We commit to fighting clean even if that means having to let go of what we hoped for. We express ourselves fully, listen to the other side, work toward agreement, and then let go. We do not use domination to make things go our way.

Whatever the outcome of a conflict is, whether positive or negative, we can always use it to learn about ourselves. Sometimes we just have to trust that things are happening for a reason, even if we can't see it immediately. We have to accept other people as they are and accept where we are ourselves. We accept the momentary outcome, knowing that there will always be another step down the track. Using what happens to learn and grow is empowering. This does not mean we should put up with destructive behaviour in others, only that things are not always the way we think they should be.

When we commit to accepting the outcome, we become less judgmental of others and of ourselves. Judgment doesn't resolve conflict, it creates it. Understanding resolves conflict.

3. Learn from the result

The third commitment is to understanding. We do this by looking deeply into ourselves and into the situation, coming to understand the meaning of our own and other people's behaviour. When we focus on understanding ourselves and other people, we have a lot more room to negotiate. We want to listen. We want to talk and express ourselves. We become interested in what is happening. What is the lesson here? How can we get it and move on? What agreement will serve both parties best?

Clean fighters care less about winning and more about learning. They are concerned with their long-term well being and the development of their own lives. They are interested in finding the right questions to ask, not in having the answers.

When we commit to understanding, we may still feel hurt and angry. But we are willing to look for the lessons even in these difficult emotions. Interestingly, as we commit to understanding, we also have less conflict in our life because we take the time and trouble to learn from each conflict. We reflect on the results, so as not to repeat the same mistakes.

Fight with clean fighters, disengage from dirty fighters

I once worked with a woman called Cindy who was breaking up with her boyfriend. He was a man who found it easy to get into relationships but almost impossible to sustain them. After they broke up, Joe continued to call Cindy. She called him back to let him know that she thought it best if they didn't attempt to be friends right now, as she needed to grieve the loss of the relationship. She took her side. But Joe actually wanted her friendship very much because he enjoyed the emotional support she provided for him, even though it was painful for her to have contact with him.

When Joe realised that Cindy was drawing a boundary and that he was not going to get what he wanted, he resorted to using dirty tactics. First he blew up in anger at her statement that she didn't want to see him right now. Then he became sarcastic, trying to wound her. Finally, he denied her point of view. Joe argued that Cindy didn't want a friendship with him because she wanted to punish him for not having been as in love with her as she had been with him.

Cindy, for her part, considered his viewpoint (took his side) and looked within to see if he was right. Did she have sour grapes? Suddenly, Cindy lost her ground. She no longer felt centred. She felt confused and lost. She had begun confidently to ask that they not see each other and now she was doubting everything she said.

She came away from the interaction feeling wounded and defeated, as if she had lost herself once again. Why had this happened? She had got caught in his dirty fighting tactics. She had fought clean (took her own side/took his side) as if they were both practising clean fighting. But they weren't. He never took her side, not even to acknowledge her need not to be friends at this time. Her error was in not noticing his dirty fighting tactics. Dirty fighters will make you feel confused and crazy.

The moral of this story is: never continue conflicting with someone who is using dirty fighting tactics. We can try to point it out to them if we suspect someone is using foul play (bullying, denial, lying, labeling, defensiveness, never taking your side, cutting you off, twisting your words). If after we have pointed out their dirty tactics, they are not willing to change their approach, we need to discontinue the conflict. It is impossible to resolve conflict with a dirty fighter. We politely express our objection to their tactics and let them know that we are unable to resolve the conflict with them at this time. And then we leave or hang up.

Cindy realised that she was a tenderhearted soul who too often took the other side, while not noticing that her side was not being honoured in return. That was an important lesson for her – to notice when dirty fighting is occurring and to disengage from it.

Don't be a hero, just fight clean

I was once part of a professional group that had a very dirty fighter in it. This woman liked a lot of attention and liked to get it by becoming attacking and belligerent. I found this most upsetting, and was annoyed at how much group energy was spent on this manipulative and difficult woman. One night I spoke up and said that I thought the way she was getting the group's attention was manipulative. As might be expected, she hit the roof. Dirty fighters tend to explode or collapse whenever someone confronts their behaviour. They deflect the truth about themselves by creating scenes.

The woman proceeded to yell at me, full force. At this point, I regret to say, I slipped into dirty fighting tactics myself. I started yelling back. I wanted to show that I wouldn't be intimidated by her yelling. Finally, she stopped. She lost face in the group. I had 'won'. I had stood up to the group bully. But I had lost. That woman never forgave me and it didn't resolve the problem. The woman continued to behave as she always did, she just felt angrier than ever.

What could I have done differently?

First of all, I should not have indulged in a yelling match. And I should not have tried to make her look bad in the group (don't hurt back).

Second, I did not need to rescue the group. I could have simply taken my side and requested that she not yell. If she hit the roof, I could have had compassion for how fearful she was of facing herself. I could have taken the conversation to a deeper level by asking the group to reflect on what was happening. I could have respectfully declined to continue the discussion. I could have spoken to her in private and not in front of the group. If all my communication attempts failed, I could have just accepted that (accept the outcome). I didn't need to solve the issue in one evening or one week.

I could have also worked on myself internally to see where I was like her and where I was getting hooked (learning from the result). I had many options, really. But I got caught in the drama of wanting to stop this woman in her tracks. I was overly attached to the outcome. I wanted to win. We all get hooked and forget our commitment to fight clean occasionally. But we learn from these mistakes and continue to grow.

Exercise: Cleaning up your act

This exercise asks you to think back upon a conflict that went badly and to review what happened from the perspective of clean and dirty fighting.

1. Recall a conflict you had with someone in which you felt badly about what happened.
2. What did you do that was dirty fighting? Why did you do that?
3. How could your fighting methods have been cleaner?
4. What did your opponent do that was dirty fighting?
5. How would you handle the conflict now?

Thoughts to hold

- Dirty fighting injures people and doesn't resolve conflict.
- Clean fighting does not harm and resolves conflict.
- If you only win, you lose; the secret to winning is to have no losers.
- Never conflict with someone who is using dirty fighting tactics.
- Commit to fighting clean by: breaking the cycle of revenge by not hurting back, accepting the momentary outcome, and learning from the results.

---

13 When Conflict Doesn't Resolve

We'll turn this thing around yet!

Jane Alexander

Sometimes we go round and round in a conflict and don't get anywhere. We are cycling, unable to move toward understanding. We stay in the loop and never find a way to resolve the problem.

Here are some symptoms of getting stuck in a conflict:
- boredom
- flat energy
- restlessness and frustration
- tiredness or exhaustion
- wishing someone was there to help you
- hopelessness, anger, hate or despair
- staring into space or feeling frozen
- both parties only taking their own side
- wanting to leave

Why do we get stuck?
There are many reasons we get stuck during conflict. Here are four common reasons people cycle in a conflict:

1. **Feeling unheard:** The most common reason for cycling is that one or both sides are unable to truly *hear* the other side. Perhaps we can't hear the other side because we still haven't expressed our own side fully enough. It is hard to hear someone if we don't feel heard ourselves. Conflicts only get resolved adequately when both sides feel heard. Until then, a conflict will continue.

2. **One or both sides wants to win more than to resolve:** Another reason for cycling is because one or both sides are unclear on the goal; they are trying to win instead of trying to reach resolution. When winning or being right is more important than resolution we never reach agreement or mutual understanding. Make sure that both sides understand the meaning of resolution: that both sides feel heard and that a solution is found that is agreeable to both people.

3. **Gatekeepers in our heads:** Sometimes a conflict will cycle because one or both parties have come to the limit of what they think they can say or do: this is the edge of our identity. We reach a personal limit and get stuck, for example, because we want to be 'nice', or 'intelligent' or 'helpful', and therefore don't express our real thoughts and feelings. Old conditioning may take over, urging us not to step over that line, not to risk new behaviours. These fears are the gatekeepers of our identity, of the status quo. They whisper, 'Nice girls don't get angry', 'No one will ever love you', 'You'll ruin everything!', 'Don't let them know what you really think!', 'If you say what you think they'll get you for it!'

   Gatekeepers *can* be wise at times. These inner inhibitors

are really trying to keep us safe and protected. But more often than not, our gatekeepers block our growth and keep us in patterns that are no longer useful. These old voices are usually not in favour of us breaking out of our self-assigned role in life and becoming our true selves. Growing and stretching can feel uncomfortable at times. But it is also freeing and exciting.

4. **Blaming:** The basic premise of conflict resolution is to eliminate blame and work towards understanding and co-operation. But it is hard to resist blaming when we feel hurt, frustrated or disappointed. Do it if you must. Get it off your chest but know that it won't work and that you will have to deal with the consequences. What are the consequences? The other side will defend themselves and launch a counter-offensive. Then you will have two sets of blame flying through the air. Blame creates blame. Break the cycle of revenge and resist blaming.

Often after we blame someone we feel guilty or regretful and try to make it better. We know deep down that blame doesn't work and aggravates the situation. Some of us never blame anyone but ourselves. This is also not helpful and leads to feelings of depression. Conflict resolution is not about self-blame or other-blame. It is about self-responsibility and requesting others to take responsibility too, to own the ways in which we have both contributed to the problem. Think in terms of contribution, not cause. We all contribute to conflict in some shape or form.

We can point out to someone when their behaviour is creating problems for us and request that they change, but we must try not to blame them by making them responsible for our feelings and problems. When we blame someone we abdicate responsibility and place it totally on another. This rarely works because there is always a piece, no matter how small, that is ours to own. And regardless of who is at fault, it usually takes both people to mend the situation. As a wonderful woman healer once said to me, 'We get what we get one by one, but we heal two by two'.

What can we do about it?

When we get stuck, we often feel defeated, depressed, exhausted, hopeless and resentful. But getting stuck is legitimate, common and human. Saying, 'We're stuck', will immediately relieve the atmosphere, clear the air and help things because we have told a truth. It is the first step towards getting unstuck. We can then try the four steps of conflict resolution again and go all the way with them.

1. **Take your own side again**: First, we need to try taking our side again, but this time more clearly, strongly or specifically. What have we left out? Have we said everything? What are we not saying? Where are we holding back or not clear about what we want? We need to be willing to go all the way, as far as we can and then some more. Both sides have an important story to tell. These stories and the telling of them create understanding, connection and ideas for resolution. Go deeper.

2. **Take the other side**: If after we have said everything we are still stuck, it may be that we are not hearing and under-

standing the other side adequately. When we refuse to see the other side, it causes them to escalate their position. They get frustrated and try to use more force in order to be understood. They get louder or meaner. Or they become silent with hopelessness. Communication becomes unproductive and even damaging if it continues this way for too long. It is vitally important to find out why we can't take the other side. Try to see where the other side is right and show your understanding of that. This has to be authentic or the other person will feel patronised. Often we do see the other's point of view but won't say so because we fear it will undermine our position. Try taking their side anyway. This usually frees up the impasse faster than anything else.

3. **Take the neutral side:** We can stand back and look at the situation as a neutral mediator. What do we see? What needs to happen next? Cycling and getting nowhere is a good time to take a look at things from the neutral side. From this vantage point we can see more easily where the communication is blocked. Many conflicts get stuck because no one is taking the neutral side and keeping the process on track.

4. **Make up:** During a conflict we may feel an impulse to reach out and be friendly to the other side. A tiny smile might flicker across our face. But we suppress it because we are 'supposed to be fighting'. Go ahead and try making up, even if there is no answer to the immediate conflict. Honour each other for trying. Apologise for any pain you have both suffered and praise each other's efforts.

Advanced tactics for when you are stuck

Sometimes repeating these steps just doesn't work. In this case, try using one of the eight advanced techniques below.

1. **Find and work on your weak spot:** When the four basic steps of conflict resolution are not enough, it is time to become aware of our personal limit, our weak spot. Where do we need to grow? Is it to take our side more strongly? Are we having trouble bringing out our emotions or needs? Are we having trouble saying something that's hard to say? Are we unable to listen? Are we too immersed in the conflict and needing to stand back and reflect on the process?

   If you are unsure about your weak spot, you can look to the other areas of your life for pointers. Usually your weak spot shows up in more than one arena. For instance, many women are not good at taking their own side right across the board. Some women tend to be opinionated and sharp-tongued and don't listen well in general. Others are too emotional and lack objectivity. Others have trouble telling the truth or expressing their anger. Others find it hard to be focused and to the point.

   Our weak spot is the area we need to develop in ourselves. It is often the thing we know we need to do but don't do because of fear, habit, discomfort or lack of confidence. We may need to work on this area in ourselves in order to resolve a conflict. Our weak spot tends to fall into one of two main categories – one of the two ends of the spectrum of human communication: not speaking up enough, or not being open to hearing others. We either withdraw into passive silence or become demanding and self-righteous. Submissive silence or dominating hostility. We give away our power or hang on to it aggressively. Which side do you tend to fall towards? The middle path of open dialogue is what's usually needed.

In moving through the three steps of conflict resolution, our side, the other side and the neutral side, we will experience our weak spot – the thing we feel unable to say, do, feel or think. These are the things that feel too hard or too much trouble to express, the things we have already decided are inappropriate, too direct, too selfish, too vulnerable or too foolish. These are the places where we say to ourselves, 'I can't do that!', 'I won't say that!' 'I feel uncomfortable doing that!', 'That's not me!', 'I'll never admit to that!'

If we know what we want to say but are afraid to express ourselves, we can first communicate our concern. We can say, 'I hate being critical and don't want to have these feelings. But I need to express a judgment here. May I proceed?' Just this much helps set the tone for discussing more difficult matters, prepares the listener and respects them by asking permission to talk about something they may find difficult.

2. **Find the energy**: Go back to the last moment of greatest energy in the conflict. Something may be incomplete there. We may have skipped over something important because it was scary or difficult. When was the last moment that felt alive and interesting? Go back to that point.

3. **Compete consciously**: Sometimes we get stuck because we just feel like being ornery and oppositional. Maybe we are

enjoying the conflict and don't really want to resolve it. Sometimes the point is to oppose one another and test our mettle. Get into the argument consciously. Try to come up with the most compelling argument. Really debate! Acknowledge when the other side scores a good point. How about brainstorming solutions together? Who can come up with the best plan for a resolution?

4. **Communicate nonverbally**: Sometimes talking just doesn't work. We can get too intellectual. Try doing something different. Try moving. Stand up and use your hands to push against each other's hands. It can be fun. Use pillows and throw them at each other. Or make sounds. Growl at one another. Do one-minute drawings of your side to show how you feel. Obviously, these suggestions will be easier to do with a partner or friend than a workmate.

5. **Accept a stalemate**: Drop the conflict. Separate and take time apart. New insights often occur when we don't feel under pressure to change. People usually resist changing under pressure. They change when no one's looking. Stalemate is an important phase of conflict resolution and should be respected. Each side should retreat. No more can be achieved for the moment. Tell your conflict partner you are finished for now but you understand the conflict is not complete and are committed to completing it when you are both ready. Some conflicts have to be dropped for months at a time because one or both sides need time to reflect privately on the issue before they can adequately work on the problem. Psychological and emotional readiness is

important. Sometimes stalemates occur because you need more information. Stop the conflict and get the information you need. Get the facts.

6. **Let go and finish up:** There is no more energy left in the conflict but you are keeping it going, like flogging a dead horse. Let go and finish up. Sometimes it is so difficult for people to enter conflict in the first place that once they do, they can't let it go. Some people can't let go because they are hooked on the adrenaline high of conflict. People hooked on conflict rarely get to the resolution stage but stay stuck in Taking Their Own Side. That is not conflict resolution. Resolution requires taking your side *and* the other side. If you or the other person hungers for the adrenaline rush of conflict, you may need professional help. Conflict and adrenaline, like any stimulant, can be addictive.

7. **Resolve it within:** Sometimes our conflict partner is too stuck to work it out with us. Release them. Forgive them for not doing better, thank them for their efforts and end the conflict on a positive note. Then separate. When you have time, work on the conflict within yourself as an inner conflict. What part of yourself does your conflict partner represent? What part of you is stuck in the way he or she is? Why are you in this conflict? What do you need to do to resolve it for yourself?

8. **Get help:** Some conflicts are too much for us to resolve without help. Admit it when you need help and make a

session with a therapist, mediator or other skilled objective third party. Needing help is healthy and normal. Some problems are long term in nature and take time to sort out. Take comfort in knowing you are doing work for the long term, even if you do not reach a resolution immediately.

Exercise: Growing beyond your weak spot

This exercise helps you to see where your weak spot is and how it keeps you stuck in conflict.

1. Think of a conflict you have had where it was hopelessly stuck, where you couldn't agree.
2. Where were you stuck personally? What was your weak spot? Did you not take your side enough? (Often this is the case, especially for women.) Or did you find it hard to listen to the other side? Most conflicts are kept active because one or both parties cannot take the other side.
3. If you took your side all the way, what would have happened? If you had supported the other side, what would have happened?
4. What old beliefs stop you from growing beyond this weak spot?
5. What new beliefs support you in growing and developing beyond your weak spot?

Thoughts to hold

- Signs of stuckness are flatness, deadness, frustration, exhaustion and hopelessness.
- Getting stuck happens when one or both parties get to their weak spot.
- Typical weak spots are: not taking our own side adequately, not listening enough or not having enough neutrality to see what's happening.
- Weak spots can become new strengths if we face them and work on them.
- Blaming creates cycling and gets us stuck. Taking responsibility gets us unstuck.
- We can get stuck if we or our conflict partner have inner problems that are holding things up. Then we need to get help or let go and resolve the issue within ourselves.
- Dirty fighting tactics also create blockages to resolution. See Chapter 12, Clean and Dirty Fighting, for more information.

14 Conclusion:
Going All the Way

All works of love are works of peace.

Mother Teresa

We have learned about the mechanics of conflict resolution such as taking our side, taking the other side, taking the neutral side and making up. We have also looked at fear and some of the issues that can exacerbate conflict, such as male and female gender roles. We have explored inner conflict and how it can eat up our energy and rob us of confidence and direction. We have addressed the issue of clean and dirty fighting. Now here is a brief summary of the entire conflict resolution process.

Acknowledge conflict

Perhaps the most important step of all is becoming aware of and being willing to acknowledge conflict. This can be a challenge in itself, because we have been trained to avoid conflict and unconsciously overlook it.

Evaluate

Having noticed that tension is present, we need to decide if it is worth tackling and, if so, how and when to address it. Some tensions are mild and inconsequential and have little impact on a relationship. Some tensions are momentary, for example, such as the tension that may arise while doing an unpleasant household task together that nobody enjoys. The tension evaporates the moment the job is done. In this case, it is not worth getting into a conflict unless there are deeper issues afoot, such as how we treat each other when stressed or frustrated. Then there are the tensions that undermine our relationships and ability to live and work together. These we should tackle.

Every relationship is unique and what is a mild conflict for one relationship may be very intense for another. What seems mild at home may seem serious in the workplace. However, when mild tensions are chronically avoided they may become serious conflicts. What was once a mere irritation can become a chronic problem and possibly a crisis down the road. Likewise, a serious issue, when worked on over time, can be transformed into an occasional mild annoyance, or disappear altogether.

Commit

Once we have decided a conflict is worth tackling, we need to make a commitment to resolving it. To do this, we need to believe that it is important, meaningful and resolvable. Many issues take time to resolve, so it is important for us to maintain our belief in change over time. Believing that things change over time can give us the energy and courage we need to commit to resolution and to persevere.

Positive beliefs

This list of beliefs can help us stay positive and committed in the midst of conflict.

- Conflict is part of life. I embrace it.
- We learn and grow through conflict.
- My conflict partner and I need each other to grow.
- Love is openness to growth and learning.
- Tension is energy waiting to be transformed.
- Great solutions come with time and practice.
- Expressing our feelings builds intimacy.
- Clean fighting means nobody gets wounded.

Whose conflict is it?

Having decided the tension is real and important, we may want to double-check to see whether to work on it internally or not. Many women err on the side of keeping things to themselves, so it is recommended to try processing tension externally until we have become experienced at it. However, we may decide it is best to work on an issue alone. For example, if it is a chronic issue and one in which both sides tend to blame each other, we may decide to work on it ourselves for the time being.

Take our own side

At some point, we will want to take our own side. When it is our turn, we bring out our feelings, needs, wants, thoughts and opinions. We are honest and direct and stick to the issue at hand. If you have trouble taking your side, say so and ask for more time, space or support to speak. Take your time and express what you have to say.

Temperature check

Here are some questions you can ask yourself after you have taken your own side.

- How do you feel having taken your side?
- How's your emotional temperature? Is it heating up or cooling down?

If you took your side fully you should be cooling down. If you are still hot, you may need to say more. The quickest way to bring down your emotional temperature is to express your side as completely as you can. After you have expressed the core of your side, your emotional temperature will drop automatically. Another way to cool down is to step out and take the neutral side.

Take the other side

When you are ready, take the other side. Listen for the essential truth or emotional core of their side. What do they want and why do they want it? When you take their side, show them your understanding and let them correct you if you are not quite getting it. When you truly get their side, their emotional temperature will cool down.

Take the neutral side: See the big picture

Having taken your side and theirs, step back from the

conflict and look at it as if from the side or above. How are things proceeding? Where are things stuck? Look at yourself and your conflict partner. Be neutral about it and not judgmental. Go back into the conflict and try to apply what you see.

Cease or cycle?

Has the conflict ceased or is it cycling? After you have taken your side, their side and the neutral side, check to see if you are spinning your wheels or resolution is in sight. Are you done? Is it over? Has the energy shifted? Has the mood improved? How is the tension level? Have you come up with ideas and options to try out? The moment you feel it is done, finish up. Don't slip into a new conflict.

If the conflict is cycling without progress, it is likely that you or your conflict partner did not take your own side completely. Go back and try taking your own sides again. Say the things that you are still holding back. Or agree to a stalemate and come back later to the issue. If this doesn't work, get help.

Share what you've learned

After you stop the process because it is resolved or you can do no more, thank each other and review what you've learned. Each person should take a moment to say what they learned about the issue at hand. This should be a brief and positive summary, even if the tension is not fully resolved. Acknowledge each other's efforts.

Resolution

At some point in the process there will be a sense of having learned something new or of understanding the situation in a new way. There is a sense of hope and co-operation. We feel greater acceptance of the other side and gratitude for their understanding. There may even be excitement about concrete strategies to try. These are all indicators that the conflict is nearing resolution. A temporary resolution is when we know there is more work to do, yet we feel things have reached a good resting place. We have made progress. Many issues are not resolved all at once but get worked out over time.

Make up and celebrate

This is the best part of all. If the conflict has been completed, even temporarily, there is a positive feeling about the progress made. Make up and celebrate! Thank each other, honour each other and reward the relationship by doing something special together: share a meal, shake hands, send a note of appreciation, hug, give flowers.

Sometimes after conflict people need some space to themselves. Allow yourselves to separate respectfully. Enjoy quiet time alone to reflect and integrate the experience. You may feel like celebrating at a later point. Whenever you are ready, do celebrate. Do not miss this step, which builds fun and pleasure into the work of conflict resolution.

Practise, Practise, Practise!

Now you have the basic tools to get into and out of conflict.

By accepting the presence of conflict and agreeing to fight clean, you have the fundamental tools for resolving conflict. Remember, it is step by step. As long as you are getting further in each conversation, you are growing in connection and understanding.

Take a moment now to do this exercise for yourself.

Exercise: Letter to yourself

Think of a conflict you worked on using one of the exercises in this book. Then write down your responses to the questions below. It doesn't matter if it is an outer or inner conflict. Put the answers in an envelope addressed to you and ask a friend or family member to mail it to you in approximately six weeks (they shouldn't tell you when they mail it. It should arrive as a surprise).

Many women tell me this letter arrives at an auspicious or meaningful moment, right when they needed the supportive reminder. You will be surprised how much you have grown in terms of the specific conflict and how you can see clearly what remains to be done.

1. What is an important conflict I worked on using one of the exercises in this book?
2. What is it about this conflict that is most difficult for me?
3. What did I learn about this conflict from doing the exercise?
4. How do I intend to integrate what I have learned into my life?
5. What is important to remember about this work on myself?

Further ideas: Pro-active learning

Here are some ideas for continuing to improve your skills:

1. Form a conflict support network among friends that focuses on learning how to resolve conflict in your lives. Set homework such as: 'This week I'm going to talk to Mike about watching television every night', or, 'I'm going to talk with my manager about wanting to change projects', or 'I'm going to listen to my sister more and see her point of view'. Phone each other for support.

2. Read books on conflict and communication. See the Bibliography for ideas.

3. Use affirmations. Stick them on your refrigerator, mirror or computer. Here are some examples:
   'I can disagree!'
   'I handle conflict with grace and ease.'
   'My side is important.'
   'Using love, I can resolve anything!'
   'I'm a great listener.'
   'I love solving problems!'

4. Get support from a therapist for deep-seated fears about conflict and interpersonal tension. Wounds from child-hood can be disempowering. Use therapy to address old wounds and restore confidence in yourself. If you find yourself in a relationship where you feel abused or domi-nated in any way, seek support from family, friends or a therapist. Consider the cost of remaining in such a damaging relationship and determine what keeps you in the relationship. You deserve to be treated with love and respect at all times. Living with someone who refuses to take joint responsibility for problems or who uses dirty

fighting tactics is not good for your health.

5. Get help in expressing yourself. Join a public speaking group such as Toastmasters. Most community colleges offer public speaking classes. This trains you to get your point across in a direct and understandable way and helps you learn to deal with questions and challenges.

6. Train to be a mediator. There are mediation and dispute resolution training centres in most cities. Use your new skills to help friends and neighbours, or volunteer as a neighbourhood mediator. The Conflict Resolution Network has a tonne of educational resources to help people deal with conflict. Contact them at: www.crnhq.org or call (612) 9419 8500.

7. Increase your multicultural awareness. Attend talks that offer information on different cultures. In most cities there are organisations that focus on international and cross-cultural issues. Becoming more sensitive to diversity provides a model for becoming sensitive to other kinds of differences in interpersonal communication, such as extroverted and introverted communication styles.

8. Educate yourself about social history and oppression. Develop an understanding of the mechanisms of racism, ethnic hostility, sexism, homophobia and international tensions and discover how your personal conflicts are connected to larger issues.

9. Practise forgiveness: When there is nothing you can do, forgive the person in your heart and know they cannot do any better right now. This cleanses you from carrying the negativity of the situation and releases you from the pattern of revenge.

10. Practise! We are all beginners when it comes to resolving conflict. Start by bringing up minor issues with people you trust. Don't stop until both parties feel enriched by the encounter and the atmosphere feels good. Ask for feedback from the other side: What did I do well? What didn't you like? Did you learn something? How could I do it better next time?

11. Support democracy and human rights in your own country and throughout the world. Remember, freedom is the right to be different.

Appendices

I Checklist: How Did I Do?

Here is a checklist of questions you can use to evaluate your skills of conflict resolution. Use the following criteria.

- Weak (*I want to strengthen this skill*)
- Fair (*I can use this skill, but not always easily*)
- Excellent (*I feel confident and comfortable using this skill*)

How did I do?	Weak	Fair	Excellent
Taking my own side			
Taking the other side			
Taking the neutral side			
Noticing escalations and de-escalations			
Dealing with accusations			
Apologising			
Making up			
Being positive and constructive			
Learning something new about myself			
Learning something new about my conflict partner			
Learning something new about the issue			
Maintaining a clean fighting style			

II A Step-by-Step Guide to Conflict Resolution

1. **Welcome:** thank both sides for agreeing to discuss the issue at hand.
2. **Communication rules:** discuss any ground rules for communication and get agreement from both sides. For example, you might agree that both sides have equal time to speak, don't cut each other off, refrain from put-downs or sarcasm, maintain confidentiality, or stick to the issue.
3. **Discussion:** let each side express their viewpoint. To get the conversation going ask open questions such as, 'Tell me how you see the issue?' or 'Let's share how we feel about this.'
   - Take your own side: state clearly how you see the issue.
   - Take the other side: listen carefully to how the other side views the issue.
4. **Take the neutral side to:**
   - Identify the issue: get both sides to agree on the main issue.

- Clarify sides: what does each side need or want in relation to the issue? What do they *not* want – or fear most?
- Recognise wins or agreements: acknowledge when agreements, insights, new understanding or learning happens.
- Recognise losses or disagreements: acknowledge where any difficulties or tensions exist.
- Recognise resolutions: acknowledge when any progress is made towards resolving the issue.

5. **Brainstorm options:** come up with ideas that meet both people's needs.
6. **Next step:** discuss what needs to happen next, if anything.
7. **Commitment:** make sure each side commits to any final decision or plan.
8. **Close:** ask each side what they gained from the discussion. Thank both sides.
9. **Celebrate!** Reward each other for tackling this issue together, even if it's not completely resolved yet.

III The Root Causes of Conflict

This section provides some ideas to help you think about conflict in its broader dimensions. You can add your own ideas to the lists below.

Power imbalances

Entrenched power imbalances are one of the primary causes of conflict. Here are some of the ways power imbalances are expressed and engender conflict:

- Injustice
- Inequality
- Inequity
- Unfairness
- Exclusion
- Exploitation
- Denial of human rights

- Discrimination (for example, racism, sexism, homophobia, anti-Semitism)
- Undemocratic practices
- Power abuses of all kinds

Individual differences

Individual differences are a fact of life and also a chief cause of conflict in our everyday lives. Having a conflict resolution framework can reduce or solve many of these conflicts between people. Here are some ways in which individuals differ:

- Values
- Opinions
- Viewpoints
- Interests
- Needs
- Wants
- Style
- Personality
- Culture

Interpersonal dynamics

Interpersonal dynamics, how we interact, are a common reason people conflict. It is often the way we treat each other that creates tension and conflict. It's not only what we say, but also how we say it. Here are some typical behaviours that cause conflict to erupt between people:

- Blaming
- Shaming

- Judging
- Condescension
- Lack of respect
- Incivility
- Belittling
- Humiliation
- Diminishing
- Not listening
- Superiority
- Aggression
- Withdrawing
- Defensiveness
- Revenge
- Using any dirty fighting tactics

Inadequate problem-solving

There is no shortage of problems in life. Many are of a practical nature. However, the way we embark on solving problems we either plant the seeds for a sustainable solution or create a larger problem down the track. Here are some causes of inadequate problem solving:

- Short-term solutions versus long-term thinking (sustainability)
- Not discovering the root cause of the problem
- Band-Aid solutions
- Not hearing everyone's viewpoint
- Intolerance of conflict or multiple viewpoints
- Lack of information or data
- Reinventing the wheel
- Lack of imagination

- Getting sidetracked by interpersonal issues (need to be addressed separately)
- Not getting help when we need it
- Not having an effective problem solving framework

Resolving strategies

These basic principles help us to solve problems and prevent damaging conflicts:

- Listening
- Inclusion
- Respect
- Multiple viewpoints
- Research
- Data, evidence and information
- Long-term thinking
- Discovering the root cause
- Ground rules
- Democratic practices
- Acceptance of difference
- Acceptance of emotion
- Upholding human rights
- Equity and fairness
- Neutral mediation
- Understanding
- Compassion
- Forgiveness
- Apology
- Acceptance
- Imagination

Bibliography

There are many general books available on conflict resolution. Here are few I have found useful:

Bach, Dr George & Wyden, Peter. *The Intimate Enemy: How to Fight Fair in Love and Marriage.* Avon Books: New York, 1968.

Bondurant, Joan. *Conquest of Violence: The Gandhian Philosophy of Conflict.* Princeton University Press: Princeton, NJ, 1958.

Burton, John (ed.). *Conflict: Resolution and Provention.* St Martin's Press: New York, 1990.

Center for Conflict Resolution. *A Handbook for Consensus Decision Making: Building United Judgment.* Center for Conflict Resolution Publications: Madison, WI, 1981.

Cornelius, Helena & Faire, Shoshana. *Everyone Can Win: How to Resolve Conflict.* Simon & Schuster: Sydney, 1989.

Crumm, Thomas. *The Magic of Conflict.* Touchstone: New York, 1987.

Eichenbaum, Luise & Orbach, Susie. *Between Women: Love, Envy and Competition in Women's Relationships.* Viking: New York, 1988.

Eichenbaum & Orbach. *What Do Women Want: Exploding the Myth of Dependency.* Berkeley Press: New York, 1983.

Elworthy, Scilla. *Power and Sex: A Book About Women.* Element Books: Dorset, 1996.

Fisher, Roger & Brown, Scott. *Getting Together: Building Relationships As We Go.* Penguin: New York, 1989.

Fisher, Roger & Ury, William. *Getting to Yes: Negotiating Agreement Without Giving In.* Penguin: New York, 1981.

Gandhi, Mahatma K. *My Experiments with Truth.* Beacon Press: Boston, 1957.

Goldman, Daniel. *Emotional Intelligence.* Bantam Books: New York, 1995.

Gottman, John with Silver, Nan. *The Seven Principles for Making Marriage Work.* Three Rivers Press: California, 2000.

Ingram, Catherine. *In the Footsteps of Gandhi.* Parallax Press: Berkeley, CA, 1990.

Larson, Jeanne & Micheels-Cyrus, Madge. *Seeds of Peace.* New Society Publishers: Philadelphia, 1987.

McAllister, Pam (ed.). *Reweaving the Web of Life: Feminism and Nonviolence.* New Society Publishers: Philadelphia, 1982.

Macy, Joanna. *World as Lover, World as Self.* New Society Press: Philadelphia, 1983.

Mindell, Arnold. *Sitting in the Fire: Large Group Transformation Using Conflict and Diversity.* Lao Tse Press: Portland, OR, 1995.

Mindell, *Leader as Martial Artist*. London: Penguin, 1989.

Norwood, Robin. *Women Who Love Too Much*. Pocket Books: New York, 1985.

Parry, Danaan. *Warrior of the Heart*. Sunstone Publications: Cooperstown, NY, 1991.

Scarf, Maggie. *Intimate Partners*. Random House: New York, 1987,

Schnarch, David. *Passionate Marriage*. Scribe Publications: Melbourne, 1997.

Smoke, Richard & Harman, Willis. *Paths to Peace*. Westview Press, Boulder, CO: 1987.

Steinem, Gloria. *Revolution From Within*. Little, Brown and Company: Boston, 1992.

Tannen, Deborah. *You Just Don't Understand: Women and Men in Conversation*. Ballantine Books: New York, 1990.

Thich Nhat Hanh. *Being Peace*. Parallax Press: Berkeley, CA, 1987.

Acknowledgments

My deepest thanks goes to the many women who have attended my conflict resolution workshops over the years. Women from all walks of life, including students, homemakers, psychologists, artists, doctors, teenagers, social activists, teachers, managers and businesswomen who have shared their stories of pain and joy in the search for sustainable resolutions. Their stories continue to enlighten and educate me about conflict, difference and human rights. I respect their contributions to the field of conflict resolution and value their efforts to resolve conflict in our world.

I also thank Drs Arny and Amy Mindell, my teachers and mentors in conflict resolution. The model of conflict resolution used in this book is based on their pioneering process-oriented conflict resolution model. I am indebted to their tireless efforts in researching conflict and providing forums for the study and application of conflict resolution throughout the world.

Many thanks to my editor Katie Stackhouse for her expert editorial assistance and belief in this book. Thanks to the entire team at Random House.

Special thanks to Lara Owen, who has been instrumental in the realisation of this work. Her professional advice and personal support has been invaluable. Many thanks also to Carol Fox for her talented assistance with the manuscript.

Thanks also to Jen Fox, Alexandra Pope, Shushann Movsessian, Ruta Cirulis, Robyn Kennedy, Anne Morphett, Kate McKnight and Paul Kennedy for their support and enthusiasm. Finally, thanks to my parents, Tom and Bette Kennedy, for their generosity and support.